LADY LIBERTY

Published by Firefly Books Ltd. 2017

First printing

Publisher Cataloging-in-Publication Data (U.S.)

Library of Congress Cataloging-in-Publication Data is available

Library and Archives Canada Cataloguing in Publication

Lebart, Luce
[Lady Liberty. English]
Lady Liberty / Luce Lebart, Sam Stourdzé.
Translation of: Lady Liberty / Luce Lebart, Sam Stourdzé. -- Paris : Seuil, 2016.
Published on the occasion of the exhibition held at the Musée départemental Arles antique, Arles, France, July 4-September 11, 2016.
Includes bibliographical references.
Contents: The idea of Liberty -- The giant's skin -- Sharing the flame -- Liberty in mind -- A Parisian construction -- The price of Liberty -- New York! -- Liberty is ours.
ISBN 978-1-77085-963-0 (softcover)
1. Statue of Liberty (New York, N.Y.)--History--Pictorial works--Exhibitions. 2. Statue of Liberty (New York, N.Y.) in art--Exhibitions. 3. Statue of Liberty National Monument (N.Y. and N.J.)--History--Pictorial works--Exhibitions. I. Stourdzé, Sam, author II. Musée départemental Arles antique, host institution III. Title. IV. Title: Lady Liberty. English
F128.64.L6L4213 2017 974.7'1 C2017-901940-6

Published in the United States by
Firefly Books (U.S.) Inc.
P.O. Box 1338, Ellicott Station
Buffalo, New York 14205

Published in Canada by
Firefly Books Ltd.
50 Staples Avenue, Unit 1
Richmond Hill, Ontario L4B 0A7

Translator: Francisation InterGlobe

Printed in China

PAGE 4

Currier and Ives, *The great Bartholdi statue, Liberty Enlightening the World : The gift of France to the American people*, 1885.
Chromolithography.
Most likely based on a drawing by the sculptor Auguste Bartholdi himself, this chromolithography is among the many anticipatory images of Liberty Enlightening the World.

We acknowledge the financial support of the Government of Canada

LADY LIBERTY

Luce Lebart
Sam Stourdzé

FIREFLY BOOKS

PUBLISHED BY CURRIER & IVES, 115 NASSAU ST. NEW YORK
Jersey City, N.J.
Hudson or North River.
NEW YORK CITY.
Castle Garden.
East River.
Brooklyn.
COPYRIGHT 1885, BY CURRIER & IVES, N
THE GREAT BARTHOLDI STATUE,
LIBERTY ENLIGHTENING THE WORLD.
THE GIFT OF FRANCE TO THE AMERICAN PEOPLE.
ERECTED ON BEDLOE'S ISLAND, NEW YORK HARBOR.
The statue is of copper-bronzed, 148 ft. in height, and is to be mounted on a stone pedestal 150 ft. high; making the extreme height 298 ft. The torch will display a powerful electric light, and the statue thus present by night as by day, an exceedingly grand and imposing appearance.

BUILDING AN ICON

★
LADY
LIBERTY
★

The power of the Statue of Liberty as an icon has greatly surpassed that of its material existence and geographical location. Initially conceived in 1865 to commemorate 100 years of American independence and to attest to the friendship between the United States and France, Lady Liberty was erected in 1886 in New York Bay, a little over 130 years ago. The origins of this impressive gift from France stem from the personal initiative and project of two men who were instrumental in its creation: the Republican jurist Édouard de Laboulaye and the Alsatian sculptor Auguste Bartholdi.

"Colossal statuary does not consist simply in making an enormous statuary," wrote Bartholdi, "but because its size is in keeping with the idea it interprets. Form is nothing without the spirit; with the idea it is everything."[1] This abstract quality, inherent to his project, would later inspire the countless appropriations and viewings of the giant statue. Doesn't offering Liberty also allow for the liberty of reinterpretation?

Thousands of images of the statue have been produced and circulated since its inauguration. Its symbolic prominence has certainly benefited from the proliferation of reproductions, whether these be touristic, promotional, propagandist, patriotic or even fantastical in nature.

The flood of images of Liberty preceded the statue's installation on American soil, a surprising fact for the period. Of the iconographic materials produced and circulated between 1865 and 1886, both in France and the United States, many were relayed by the burgeoning illustrated press. The construction of the Statue of Liberty was also a true media phenomenon, which began an unprecedented relationship between the statue and its image, between liberty and photography.

1. Auguste Bartholdi, *Colossi of Memnon*, Thebes, Egypt, 1856. Albumenized salt print, 9.7" × 7.5" (24.6 × 19.1 cm).

It comes as no surprise to discover that Bartholdi the sculptor was also a photographer. During the mid-1850s, when he was 20 years old, Bartholdi indulged in this medium and even became a pioneer in photography, only to leave it later in favor of painting and sculpting. He produced an impressive photographic documentation of his personal history, such as his voyage to the United States in 1871, during which he likely began to envision where he would place his colossus on Bedloe's Island. These photographs also show his fascination with modern monumental structures made of iron and steel, such as viaducts and railways — products of cutting-edge engineering. These refer back to his first salted paper prints, which attest to the young sculptor's taste for colossal Egyptian architecture *(Fig. 1):*

> "We are filled with awe in the presence of these colossal displays, several centuries old, from a past that seems to us infinitely far away and at the feet of which so many generations, millions of lives, and so much human glory was swept away to dust. To

> this day, these granite beings, in their unflappable splendor, seem to refer back to the furthest recesses of antiquity. Their stolid and authoritarian gazes seem to ignore the present and be fixated on a future that seems without limits."[2]

A photographic commission would become the catalyst for his trip to the Middle East. "Misters A. Bartholdi and Gérôme *(Fig. 2)* were tasked with studying Egyptian, Nubian and Palestinian relics, as well as photographing these countries' major monuments and their most striking people."[3] Bartholdi was clearly inspired by his visit, as demonstrated by the albumen prints that detail his sketches for his Liberty's base, the majority of which are pyramid shaped *(Fig. 3)*. Yet this would ultimately not be the shape of the final design. The task of its creation would be entrusted, in 1881, to the American architect Richard Morris Hunt, already famous for having built the *New York Tribune* building in 1876 — one of New York's first skyscrapers.

2. *Auguste Bartholdi and a Fellow Traveler* (probably Jean-Léon Gérôme), Egypt, 1856. Salted paper print, 10" × 7" (25.5 × 17.8 cm).

"Auguste is taking photography classes," his mother wrote on July 30, 1854. Bartholdi, who was close to the painter Jean-Léon Gérôme, may have been under the tutelage of Gustave Le Gray, a photography teacher also acquainted with Gérôme. Le Gray initiated Maxime Du Camp, author of the famous 1852 work *Egypt, Nubia, Palestine and Syria*, which detailed a trip that he undertook with Flaubert, similar to Bartholdi's own journey. Bartholdi used the same dry waxed paper technique that was perfected by Le Gray during his travels. Thus, Bartholdi followed in Du Camp's footsteps, yet he also followed Salzmann, an Alsatian himself, whose calotypes of Jerusalem won second place at the Exposition Universelle held in Paris in 1855.

3. Pierre Petit, *Reproduction of a Sketch of the Pedestal Project for the Statue of Liberty* 1881–1884. Albumen print.

As well as taking photographs, Bartholdi also liked to collect them, as shown by his large collection, in which several important names associated with the still image — Disdéri, Nadar, Le Secq, Désiré, Goupil and Hammerschmidt — can be found.[4] He documented his own works, particularly the project *Liberty Enlightening the World*, through photographs. To do this, Bartholdi turned to professional photographers, such as his friend Pierre Petit, and also purchased his contemporaries' images. Photographs documenting the progress on building and restoration sites *(Figs. 4 and 5)* were at that point common practice, particularly for bridges and roadways. Viollet-le-Duc, a member of the Franco-American Union to which Bartholdi had entrusted the construction of his statue prior to Gustave Eiffel's role in its completion, theorized and elucidated in his architectural dictionary the necessity of photographing the various restoration stages.

The "Plomberie et cuivrerie d'art" [plumbing and copper smelting] facilities of Monduit and Béchet (Gaget and Gauthier's successors), located in Paris on rue de

LEFT

4. Pierre Petit, *The Statue of Liberty's Foot: Inside the Gaget Gauthier Workshop*, 1882. Albumen print on blue cardboard, 10.1" × 7.7" (25.7 × 19.5 cm) and 12.2" × 8.6" (30.9 × 21.8 cm).

ABOVE

5. Pierre Petit, *Gaget, Gauthier & Co. Workshop: The Construction of the Statue of Liberty*, 1882. Albumen print mounted on cardboard, 10.1" × 7.6" (25.6 × 19.3 cm) and 17.3" × 13.5" (43.9 × 34.4 cm).

Chazelles, were designated as the location for building the giant. There would be a four-year gap between the installation of the first rivet and the completion of the Parisian construction. The following photographs record the iron spine's climb toward the sky. This task was carried out by Gustave Eiffel, who continued the work after Viollet-le-Duc passed away in 1879. The photographs are signed by Pierre Petit and Albert Fernique, the latter being a professional photographer specializing in "photographing the works of engineers and architects." These famous shots of the 151-foot (46 m) copper statue overlooking Parisian roofs attest to all the changes taking place, including those occurring in the background such as the buildings under construction, with paneless and shutterless windows, sprouting just as slowly. The years taken to build Liberty were also times of change for Haussmann's Paris. Construction was reaching an end and the journalists were impressed. Among them was André Michel, who wrote in July 1884:

> "This colossal work, conceived during one of those moments of ardent enthusiasm when the artist happily challenges all the difficulties and material impossibilities and senses, from the bottom of his heart, the union between the will and the marvelous dream. She's been looming over Paris for a few weeks now, and is at the center of the city's deepest rumors, waiting for the moment when the ocean rocks her gently with its waves, caressing her with its breezes and chanting with its strong yet gentle and never-ending whispers."[5]

Pierre Petit, also a member of the Franco-American Union, documented the various worksite stages. He recorded the production of the wooden preliminary structures, the making of the templates, the life-sized plaster models and the behind-the-scenes work on the wrought copper. Petit, who trained in the studio of Eugène Disdéri — the man who invented the photographic business card and is considered to be the first fixed-image manufacturer — also helped the sculptor to reproduce his documentation. He photographed his drawings, models and projects and produced them as albumen prints, of which he made several copies.

Charles Marville, a photographer of the city of Paris, began to work alongside Pierre Petit. Although he passed away in 1879, the same year as Viollet-le-Duc, Marville nevertheless had the opportunity to immortalize through photography Liberty's plaster head before its copper casing was installed. This also included the time it was displayed during the 1878 Exposition Universelle in the Champs de Mars park.

Bartholdi used all this photographic documentation for his research when visualizing his projects on their future sites. He did not hesitate to draw or paint directly on the photographs, or to cut and paste them to create a kind of photomontage sketch. He also helped fund a giant panorama of the New York Bay when the Brooklyn Bridge was first being built (see inside cover photograph), and used this as a backdrop when envisioning the placement of his future Liberty. He even went so far as to cut out Liberty's head and place it perfectly at the entrance of the 1878 Exposition Universelle, imagining it on the front page of a famous illustrated newspaper. The sculptor then worked with and from these images, molding and manipulating them, something he also did with the grounds sketches. He would deform and reduce them, only to create a new form.

Auguste Bartholdi readily offered his images to journalists and editors. Before 1886, reproducing photographs in newspapers or magazines required the engraver to redraw the image to fit in with the paper's layout *(Figs. 6, 7 and 8)*.

6. Karl Fichois, *Building the Statue of Liberty*, 1885. Lead pencil drawing.

7. Pierre Petit (based on his own photograph), *The Hand of the Statue of Liberty, by M. Bartholdi*, in *L'Illustration*, Paris, December 9, 1882. Printed engraving.

8. Narcisse Navellier and Alexandre Léon Marie, based on the photographs of Pierre Petit, *Work on the Statue*, engraving featured in *Notice, Documents on the Work of the Franco-American Union*, 1883. Brochure published by *Le Journal illustré*, 1884. Engraving, centerfold, 15.7" × 11.4" (40 × 29 cm).

This photograph-based drawing technique was used by *L'Illustration* magazine in 1843, the year of its launch. American illustrated journals like *Harper's Weekly* (1857–1916) and *Frank Leslie's Illustrated Newspaper* (1855–1922), which were launched at a later date, published these images from 1861. Although all used identical snapshots, the panels sometimes varied from one publication to another, depending on the interpretation of the engraver who, either at the sculptor's, photographer's or paper's request, or through his own initiative, would add figures and emphasize or minimize certain details. This was the case with Liberty's plaster head in the Gaget Workshop and the retouched photographic templates that showed the preparatory work.

Liberty's first public picture appeared in 1875 in two journals, *L'Illustration* on Saturday, October 9 and *Le Journal illustré* on Sunday, October 10. The engravings were based on photographs by Pierre Petit that were themselves based on Bartholdi's drawing, most likely prior to 1875. This anticipatory drawing, closely resembling the real thing (other than its pedestal), depicted the statue on its New York site, with luminous rays shining from its diadem. Recalling the preparatory drawings of his uncompleted project *Egypt Bringing Light to Asia*, these rays also inspired the shape of the statue's future pointed diadem. It was ultimately the version in *Harper's Weekly* — one that was reproduced in several newspapers, such as *Le Journal illustré* on Saturday, November 27, 1875 — that was the closest to the final model *(Fig. 9)*.

Édouard de Laboulaye, during the November 6, 1875, banquet — the first important promotional event aimed at gaining and boosting the press's and politicians' attention — underscored a difficulty: the colossal statue's location. He referenced Munich's famous *Bavaria*, which was placed in a field, stating, "We don't know why it's there rather than someplace else." In fact, the image of the statue *in situ* before the immense cities of New York, Brooklyn and Jersey City was the first to be published by the press.

Liberty's illustrated chronicles become the types of images most sought after by the press. As dictated by the period's taste for the biographies of famous figures, Bartholdi would see his own portrait time and again *(Figs. 10 and 11)*. Other popular themes were the celebration of the day-to-day, or events with a commemorative or patriotic feel. From the statue's construction launch at the rue

Le Journal illustré

DOUZIÈME ANNÉE — N° 41

Gravures :
La statue de la Liberté, par H. Meyer. — *Le nouveau Pont et la Percée du boulevard Saint-Germain*, par Karl Fichot. — *L'Éclipse partielle de soleil, vue prise au Pont-Neuf*, par Henri Meyer et Georges Guiaud. — *L'Inondation de Saint-Chinian*, par Georges Guiaud. — *L'Enfant du Faubourg*, par Henri Meyer.

DIMANCHE 10 OCTOBRE 1875

Le Journal illustré est mis en vente dès le vendredi matin

ABONNEMENT	UN AN	SIX MOIS
Paris	6 50	3 50
Départements	7 50	4 .

Administration & Rédaction, à Paris, hôtel du Petit Journal, rue de Lafayette, 61.

PRIX DU NUMÉRO : 15 CENTIMES

Texte :
Chronique de la semaine, par Aristide Roger. — *Beaux-Arts et Théâtres*, par Charles Darcours. — *La statue de la Liberté*. — *Robert Favraz*, roman inédit, par Emile Desbeaux. — *Sonnet*, par Ch. de Bourbonne. — *La Vengeance du Carrier*, par Robert Glam. — *L'Inondation de Saint-Chinian*, par J. de L. — *Nos illustrations de l'Enfant du Faubourg*, le roman du *Petit Journal*, par G. Clere. — *Mot carré et Devineurs.*

La Statue de la Liberté

QUI DOIT ÊTRE OFFERTE A L'AMÉRIQUE PAR LA FRANCE ET ÉLEVÉE DEVANT NEW-YORK

Dessin de Henri Meyer d'après les photographies de Pierre Petit — Voir les détails, page 323

9. Based on Pierre Petit's photograph, ***The Statue of Liberty that France Must Offer to the United States Is Raised Before New York*****, in** ***Le Journal illustré*****, 12th year, No. 41, October 10, 1875. Printed engraving, 7.3" × 8.9" (18.5 × 22.5 cm).**

de Chazelles workshop *(Fig. 12)* up until its American unveiling, with numerous banquets, shows, operas, dinners and get-togethers organized by the Franco-American Union meant to help finance the work on the statue through the use of subscriptions among other things, there was no shortage of opportunity to immortalize Lady Liberty. In addition to this was the appeal of a utopian idea made possible, and the appreciation for the achievement of such an such an impressive technical feat. The materials and innovative procedures used for Bartholdi's project drew on the most advanced technology then available. The dimensions of the various parts were often cited, from the length of a finger to the size of the head:

> The hand is five meters [16 feet] long, with the index finger measuring two meters forty-five [8 feet], with a circumference of one meter forty-four [4 feet 8 inches] at the second phalanx. As for the nail, it is thirty-three centimeters by twenty-six [13" × 10¼"]. The Statue of Liberty was, without a

doubt, the most colossal work of its kind ever to have been created. Not including its pedestal, the statue would surpass by 2 meters 8 centimeters [6 feet 10 inches] the height of the Place Vendôme column, which measured forty-four meters [144 feet] from base to tip. Forty people could stand inside its head (4.4 m [14 feet 5 inches]), while at least 12 could fit in the torch.[6]

10. Henri Meyer, based on Pierre Petit's photograph, Mr. *Auguste Bartholdi, Statuary*, in *Le Journal illustré*, 20th year, No. 20, May 13, 1883. Printed engraving, 9.8" × 8.9" (25 × 22.8 cm).

FAR RIGHT 11. Paul Nadar, *Portrait of Bartholdi, in Galerie contemporaine*, No. 24. Patin Photoglyptie 6.1" × 4.3" (15.5 × 11 cm), on the journal cover, 14.8" × 10.8" (37.5 × 27.5 cm).

Bartholdi, always with the Franco-American Union's backing, contributed in the promotion of his project — with the help of journalists and editors — by organizing exhibitions and conferences, and even hosting a dinner inside the sculpture's leg when it was erected in the heart of Paris. The involvement of certain journalists, including *New York World* owner Joseph Pulitzer, transformed the statue's destiny in 1885: "Money must be found at all costs," Pulitzer wrote in his newspaper, viewed as a mouthpiece for the everyman. The halt on the pedestal's building site caused Lady Liberty to become a popular subject for American caricaturists, who mocked this setback by depicting the statue as aging and exhausted, waiting for a financial resolution. *Life* featured her on its January 17, 1884, cover with a drawing entitled, "The Statue of Liberty as It Will Be Once the Pedestal is Completed," while on August 30 *Frank Leslie's Illustrated Newspaper* showed Liberty, bent and decrepit, sitting on the unfinished pedestal "A Thousand Years Later And Still Waiting."

With the arrival of illustrated advertisements, a development contemporaneous with the New York statue, the effigy and its image went through a variety of transformations — substitutions that are still used today. The torch

12. Based on Pierre Petit's photograph *The United States Ambassador, Mr. Morton, Installs the First Rivet, in Harper's Weekly,* December 3, 1881. Printed engraving, 10.1" × 8.5" (25.7 × 21.7 cm) excluding margins.

would suffer the most satire, from being replaced with a light bulb (1883) to medicines (1886), with an umbrella and sewing thread in between. Before the pedestal was even completed, the amount of publicity received was such that the magazine *Puck* suggested, on April 8, 1885, to "leave the advertisers in charge of Bartholdi's business and money will immediately be found." Clad in sunglasses and holding a bottle of champagne instead of the tablet of law, the statue is bedecked with slogans boasting of the merits of cigarettes, bitters, beer and more.

However, the illustrated press and advertisers were not the only sources reproducing images of *Liberty Enlightening the World*. These circulated through a variety of media. Some were found in dioramas, where the marriage of images and theater created a popular visual show, very much in vogue since the 1870s.

> "Through who knows what kind of extraordinary trompe-l'oeil, one finds oneself suddenly transported to the back of an American liner that seems to leave the New York Bay, all while on the bridge, close by, life-sized models talk and smoke [...]. All around us

> we hear the ocean that is boiling and agitated [...], an incredible amount of motion, when here is the island the middle of which [...] we see rising, superb, grandiose, illuminating the world with its electric beacon — the giant Statue of Liberty."[7]

A paid show, this illusory panorama, called "View of New York Bay and the commemorative monument of the friendship between France and the United States," is a painted semicircular canvas, measuring 36.1 feet (11 m). It was located in the Jardin des Tuileries during the 1878 Exposition Universelle. The colored ads announcing it in Paris were signed by the "father" of the advertising poster, Jules Chéret. Success was in the cards for the event, as no fewer than 7,000 entries were counted in two months.

The scenography also held a place of honor during the November 6, 1875, banquet of the Franco-American Union. The apparatus was something spectacular for the period; a model of Liberty was placed at the center of the head table while, on the wall across from it, a "large projection" grabbed everyone's attention. In fact, it was Bartholdi himself who collaborated with Pierre Petit to create the ingenious luminous screen that reproduced the future monument.

But the sculpture's creator didn't stop there: he displayed his whole studio under the guise of a genuine visual spectacle. As of March 1878, the head's building site was open to some curious souls. It was only by the end of 1882, however, that Bartholdi would admit the general public to the site on Mondays and Thursdays from noon until 5 p.m. — as long as they had admission tickets. According to Philibert Bréhan's piece in the March 6, 1878 *Le XIXe Siècle*, it was one of the strangest sights to behold:

> "Yesterday, we were entertained for over two hours, without getting bored. Mr. Bartholdi and his helpers were putting the final touches on the statue: one, standing on the first scaffolding level, fixed the mouth; a second, on the next level, retouched the eyes; the third, at the top level, detailed the diadem, which crowns this giant figure. Carpenters were placing pieces of wooden planks to cover the statue with a kind of wooden mask. Once these frames were finished, they were placed on the floor, the

> outlined face turned towards the sky, after which it was covered in copper that was in turn molded to fit wood. With the help of mallets, hammers, scissors and steel spikes, the copper plaque was inserted into the wooden mold, which formed the mask's different parts, to be welded together later. This process ensures a faithful reproduction of the head."

The statue's disassembly and crating would also become an attraction a few months later: "All that can be heard are the hammer blows, grinding stones, the clank of chains — everywhere movements, chaos. You'd think it was a huge factory."

Rising above the capital's rooftops, the model statue could also be climbed for a fee. The torch, transported in 1876 to Philadelphia and New York, could also be visited, as could the head, which was made open to the public in 1878 during the Exposition Universelle in Paris. In fact, *Le Monde illustré* entered the dialogue with its sketch of the head's interior in its September 28, 1878, publication. The writer Rudyard Kipling wrote of his pleasure at being able to climb into the head *(Fig. 13)*:

> "A feature of [the Exposition] was the head of Bartholdi's Statue of Liberty which, later, was presented to the United States. One ascended by a staircase [...] to the dome of the skull and looked out through the vacant eye-balls at a bright-coloured world beneath. I climbed up there often [...]"[8]

The statue was placed between the buildings on rue de Chazelles in a kind of scaffold corset — such was the image that would be immortalized by the engraver Tilly for the April 5, 1884, edition of *L'Illustration*. And such was its condition when Victor Hugo and his granddaughter made a visit to the monument and its sculptor. "Two giants watching one another," observed French banker Henri Cernuschi of the encounter between Liberty and Hugo, and the writer stated: "The ocean, that greatly disquieted being, is what unites these two great and peaceful lands". Moved, Bartholdi offered a piece of the statue to this French literary giant, with the inscription, "To Victor Hugo, from the Franco-American Union. A fragment from the colossal Statue of Liberty presented to the apostle for peace, liberty

LE MONDE ILLUSTRÉ

JOURNAL HEBDOMADAIRE

ABONNEMENTS POUR PARIS ET LES DÉPARTEMENTS
Un an, 24 fr. ; — Six mois, 13 fr. ; — Trois mois, 7 fr. ; — Un numéro, 35 c.
Le volume semestriel, 12 fr. broché. — 17 fr., relié et doré sur tranche.
LA COLLECTION DES 21 ANNÉES FORME 42 VOLUMES.
Directeur, M. PAUL DALLOZ.

BUREAUX
13, QUAI VOLTAIRE
22e Année: No 1122 — 28 Sept. 1878

DIRECTION ET ADMINISTRATION, 13, QUAI VOLTAIRE
Toute demande d'abonnement non accompagnée d'un bon sur Paris ou sur la poste, toute demande de numéro à laquelle ne sera pas joint le montant en timbres-poste, seront considérées comme non avenues. — On ne répond pas des manuscrits envoyés.
Administrateur, M. BOURDILLIAT. — Secrétaire, M. E. HUBERT.

LES COULISSES DE L'EXPOSITION. — Dans la Tête de la statue de la *Liberté* au Champ-de-Mars. — (Dessin de M. Oms.)

13. F. Moller, based on a drawing by M. Oms, *The Exposition Wings — Inside the Head of the Statue of Liberty at Champ-de-Mars,* in *Le Monde illustré,* 22nd year, No. 1122, September 28, 1878. Printed engraving, 10.6" × 8.3" (26.8 × 21 cm).

and progress, Victor Hugo, on the day he honored us with his visit to the Franco-American Union's work."

The exhibition of the two sections (head and torch) became a business opportunity: souvenirs, badges, small-scale models and photographs were all sold at the statue's base. Pierre Petit's photograph of the model was reproduced as a photoglypty (a photo-mechanical process invented by Goupil, father-in-law to the painter Gérôme) and was distributed in the thousands as of 1884. If the rightful ownership of these products cannot be directly attributed to Bartholdi and his team, the statue's commercialization — its marketing (to use a current term) — helped create an alternative financial resource, the scale of which had no predecessors (Walt Disney would be the next to harness it as successfully). This ultimately placed the image at the forefront and created a direct link to sales of merchandise. This advertising model was a precursor to what is common practice today.

Liberty's 20 years of construction sites were recorded by the illustrated press as much as was the Expositions Universelles. During those golden years, the two events were just as cutting-edge as development of photography in the the illustrated newspapers. In fact, the Exposition universelle de 1867 in Paris was also an occasion to discover just how much the field of photography had progressed. Photos of the "Egyptian Park," as conceived by the archeologist Pierre Mariette were widely published. Not far from the Egyptian Pavilion, home to the plaster model of Bartholdi's Statue of Champollion, was the "Isthmus of Suez," which was presented by its project manager, the engineer Ferdinand de Lesseps. De Lesseps was also a member of the committee tasked with collecting subscriptions for the creation of the Statue of Champollion and was the future president of the Franco-American Union for Liberty Enlightening the World. The giant-sized plan and hydraulic machines used during Ferdinand de Lesseps' project were fascinating to the young sculptor. From that moment, he dreamed of a colossal-sized statue. This dream took the shape of a statue of a woman draped in fabric with an arm reaching toward the sky. Bartholdi conceived it as Egypt Bringing Light to Asia and to be placed at the mouth of the famous Suez Canal.

It was a modified version that was ultimately offered to the United States, of which Bartholdi's Egypt was undoubtedly the draft. By moving his statue from the East to the West, Bartholdi could not have fathomed just how premonitory his project turned out to be. This change would herald the arrival of the 20th century as well as the American domination, when the New World was to assert itself in international relations, industrial power and liberty.

1. Auguste Bartholdi, *The Statue of Liberty Enlightening the World*, New York, North American Review, 1885. Re-edited and reprinted with an introduction by Jeffrey Eger, New York, New York Bound, 1984, p. 40.

2. Auguste Bartholdi quoted by Pierre Provoyeur, "The Idea and the Form," *The Statue of Liberty: Centennial Exhibition*, Paris, Musée des Arts Décoratifs / Selections from the Reader's Digest, 1986, p. 94.

3. National Archives (France), F17/2935/2.

4. Hammerschmidt's collection of photographs is kept at the Musée Bartholdi in Colmar, France.

5. André Michel, "The Statue of Liberty Lighting Bartholdi's World," *Revue alsacienne*, July 1884, pp. 385–88.

6. "The Hand of the Statue of Liberty by Mr. Bartholdi, given to the City of New York and Constructed in Paris," *L'Illustration*, December 9, 1882.

7. Undated newspaper clipping, CNAM Library, No. 652. See Catherine Hodeir's "The French Campaign" in *The Statue of Liberty, The Centennial Exhibition, op. cit.*, p. 145. "

8. Rudyard Kipling, *Memories of France*, Paris, Grasset, 1933, pp. 25–26.

AN ILLUSTRATED HISTORY

★ LADY LIBERTY ★

Auguste Bartholdi, the creator of the statue *Liberty Enlightening the World*, credited a dinner in 1865 with the monument's conception. The friendship ties between France and the United States were threaded by Republican Édouard de Laboulaye. He suggested, to commemorate 100 years of American independence, building "in joint effort" a monument that would be "a common work between two nations."

This idea sparked something in the young sculptor, who had discovered the Middle East during an exploratory trip undertaken in 1855 with the painter Jean-Léon Gérôme. It is with Egypt and its Pharaonic monuments in mind that Bartholdi created the sketches, in 1867, for a project of which the shape and concept bring to mind his Liberty. His giant statue, called *Egypt (Progress) Bringing Light to Asia*, is a woman draped in fabric, clad in a veil and holding up a torch. Dreaming of erecting it at the entrance of the Suez Canal, Bartholdi presented his sketches to his proponent Ferdinand de Lesseps and the Khedive Ismaïl Pacha in 1869, but was unsuccessful. However, the sculptor followed the advice of the latter, who said he "would rather see the light apparatus worn on the head, as in the style of a female fellah." This served as inspiration for Bartholdi, who drew the first beacon statue with luminous rays emanating from its head and lighting the horizon.

Auguste Bartholdi, *Suez Lighthouse Project*, 1869. Watercolor over graphite pencil sketch, 7.9" × 5.5" (20 × 14 cm). *Egypt Bringing Light to Asia*, Auguste Bartholdi's beacon-statue project, with a light in hand in the style of the Colossus of Rhodes, was intended to rise at the Suez Canal entrance. The sculptor's watercolors and clay models reveal various attempts with poses, the positioning of the hips and draping. Clad in a veil, Egypt was already wearing the diadem that would become the Statue of Liberty's. Its giant pedestal copied that of the Lighthouse of Alexandria.

The Idea of Liberty

Unknown author, *Reproduction of Auguste Bartholdi's Drawing for the Suez Lighthouse Project as Presented to the Khedive*, 1869. Albumen print, 3.3" × 2.3" (8.5 × 5.8 cm). This albumen photograph is a copy of a drawing or watercolor that was annotated on the mounting board by the sculptor; "Suez Lighthouse Project, presented to the Khedive in 1869." Although it is lost now, Bartholdi mentions it in his correspondence: "I presented my statue model and drawings to the viceroy. He looked at them with interest." Egypt was shown from the front, wearing a necklace and baring her chest. Just as Liberty would later be posed, Egypt's raised arm held a flaming torch. Yet the light was not emanating from the flame, but rather from the diadem in a style similar to that of the Lighthouse of Alexandria. The image of the statue of *Liberty Enlightening the World* as depicted in the preparatory drawings, also front-facing, was distributed initially to promote the project.

Auguste Bartholdi, *Pyramidal Pedestal Project for Liberty Enlightening the World, Scale of 0.005 thousand pm*, circa 1880. Graphite pencil and wash on glued paper, 20" × 14.2" (51.× 36 cm).
As the project's origins were a collaboration between France and the United States, the American architect Richard Morris Hunt was entrusted with the development of the pedestal. This did not stop Bartholdi from imagining various projects with the recurring motif of the pyramid, a testament to his fascination with the country so skilled in creating colossal architecture.

Pierre Petit, *Reproduction of an Auguste Bartholdi Painting of the Statue of Liberty in New York Bay*, 1881–1884. Albumen print, 6.6" × 9.5" (16.8 × 24.2 cm). Auguste Bartholdi had copies made of his drawings and watercolors as a means of promoting his project. His friend Pierre Petit, a famous photographer known for his eccentricity, signed the majority of the albumen prints, often yellowed with time. Here, the Statue of Liberty is posed in a similar manner to that shown in the photograph of *Egypt Bringing Light to Asia*. However, she is holding the tablet of law and is not wearing a fellah-style veil. The project's instigator would, in 1876, describe her as being "Liberty, but the American liberty. It is not liberty with a red cap on her head and a pike in hand who walks on corpses. Ours holds in one hand a torch, not a torch that burns but one that lights the way, and in the other the tables of law."

Anticipated view of *Liberty Enlightening the World* from New York Bay.
Anticipatory engraving of the Statue of Liberty on its Bedloe's Island site, reproduced by photoglypty. Franco-American Union. Speech by Misters Henri Martin, E.B. Washburne, Édouard Laboulaye and J.W. Forney during the Franco-American banquet on November 6, 1875, in Paris.

RIGHT PAGE

Pierre Petit, *Reproduction of an Auguste Bartholdi Drawing Depicting the Statue of Liberty in New York Bay,* 1881–1884.
Albumen print, 7.3" × 10.1" (18.5 × 25.7 cm).
Using a negative photomask placed on a glass plaque, Pierre Petit created several copies of a single image as drawn by Bartholdi. These copies were then sent to anyone who could help sustain and promote the monument, particularly journalists. This anticipatory image of the Statue of Liberty placed in New York Bay was disseminated most often as a printed engraving, during a time when the illustrated newspaper medium was growing. The *L'Illustration* engraver has here even taken the time to detail all the little boats that were featured in Bartholdi's initial drawing.

C. Muran, based on an Auguste Bartholdi drawing, *Commemorative Monument Project to be Erected at the Entrance of the New York Bay, on the Occasion of the Centennial of the Independence of the United States*, in *L'Illustration*, No. 1702, October 9, 1875, p. 229.
Printed engraving, 5.9" × 8.7" (15 × 22.2 cm).

Projet de monument commémoratif a élever a l'entrée de la baie de New-York, a l'occasion du centenaire de l'Indépendance des États-Unis.
D'après le dessin original de M. Bartholdi, statuaire.

Auguste Bartholdi, *Anticipated Views of the Statue of Liberty, New York Bay*, 1883–1884. Watercolor on paper, 5.8" × 8.9" (14.8 × 22.8 cm); 5.7" × 9.6" (14.4 × 24.3 cm); 5.5" × 8.7" (14 × 22 cm); 6.1" × 9.6" (15.5 × 24.3 cm).

Bartholdi would create numerous watercolor sketches of the statue at the Bay even before its pedestal was built. The water dotted with boats guided by the winds, the sea changes, like the clouds, just as the colossus's copper changes color in the light.

Financing would still be an issue when work began in Paris in 1875 at the large plumbing and copper smelting workshops of Monduit and Béchet — successors to Gaget and Gauthier — who were located behind Parc Monceau.

To ensure his statue's stability, Auguste Bartholdi worked alongside the architect and restorer, Eugène Viollet-le-Duc, who would suggest technical solutions. Copper was preferred to bronze to create the giant's skin. In what looked like a giant factory, carpenters, plaster sculptors, blacksmiths, boilermakers and braziers were working based on a plaster model that measured 6 feet 11 inches (2.11 m) in height, the equivalent of 1/16 of the actual size.

For each enlarged part of the statue, a wooden structure was created that would later be covered in plaster, and would serve to help position the wooden frames. These then became the molds for the 300 fine sheets of copper that were hammered into the shape of the statue's golden skin.

Bartholdi, with the idea of helping to finance the project, opened the construction site to the public for a fee. He also called on photographers — professionals such as Pierre Petit, Charles Marville and Albert Fernique— who immortalized the stages of the construction.

Pierre Petit, *Gaget, Gauthier & Co. Workshop: Construction of the Statue of Liberty*, Paris, 1881–1884. Albumen print on cardboard, 7.6" × 10" (19.2 × 25.5 cm) and 11.4" × 13.8" (29 × 35 cm), respectively.
On the left-hand side of the photograph, Auguste Bartholdi, whom we recognize thanks to his beard and white shirt, inspects the 300 copper pieces that will envelop his colossal statue.

The Giant's Skin

PAGES 40–41

Anonymous (attributed to Pierre Petit). *Gaget, Gauthier & Co Workshop: Construction of the Statue of Liberty*, Paris, 1881–1884. Albumen print, 10.1" × 13.1" (25.7 × 33.4).
A true-to-size plaster model was created by the Gaget and Gauthier workshop sculptors. Here are the bust and the left arm holding the tablet of law. These plasters would later help in the creation of the wooden jigs that would in turn be used during the hammering of the fine copper plaques.

PAGES 42–43

Pierre Petit, Gaget, *Gauthier & Co.: Construction of the Statue of Liberty*, Paris, 1881–1884. Albumen print, 7.3" × 10" (18.6 × 25.3 cm).
The plasters were created from a wood and lath structure. This form was itself created by enlarging a model that was 16 times smaller. The principal points that were then obtained were joined together by the lath work. The wooden structure was then covered in plaster.

Pierre Petit (attributed to), *Gaget, Gauthier & Co. Workshop: Construction of the Statue of Liberty*, Paris, 1881–1884. Albumen print, 7.7" × 10.1" (19.6 × 25.7 cm).
Based on the true-to-size plaster models, the wooden jigs were used in the construction of the copper pieces that would become its covering. The statue's giant finger can be seen in the middle of the photograph. It would be displayed, as of 1877, alongside the diorama at the Palace of Industry.

La fonte de la statue de la « Liberté

Dessin de Karl FICI

Bartholdi dans les ateliers Thiébaut

· l'article, page 155.

PREVIOUS PAGES

Karl Fichot, “The Melting of the Statue of ‘Liberty’ by Mr. Bartholdi in the Thiébaut Workshop,” *Le Journal illustré,* May 17, 1885.

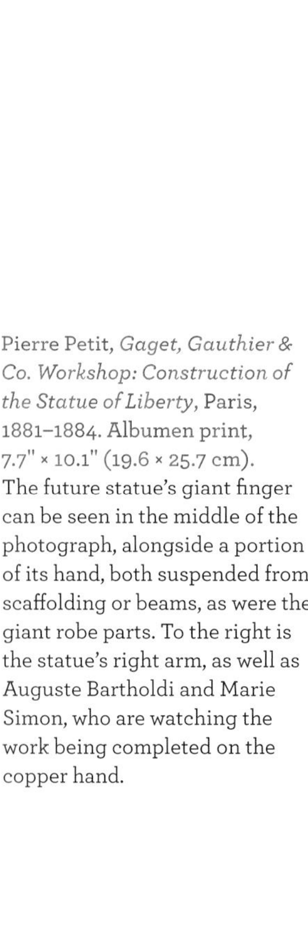

Pierre Petit, *Gaget, Gauthier & Co. Workshop: Construction of the Statue of Liberty*, Paris, 1881–1884. Albumen print, 7.7" × 10.1" (19.6 × 25.7 cm). The future statue’s giant finger can be seen in the middle of the photograph, alongside a portion of its hand, both suspended from scaffolding or beams, as were the giant robe parts. To the right is the statue’s right arm, as well as Auguste Bartholdi and Marie Simon, who are watching the work being completed on the copper hand.

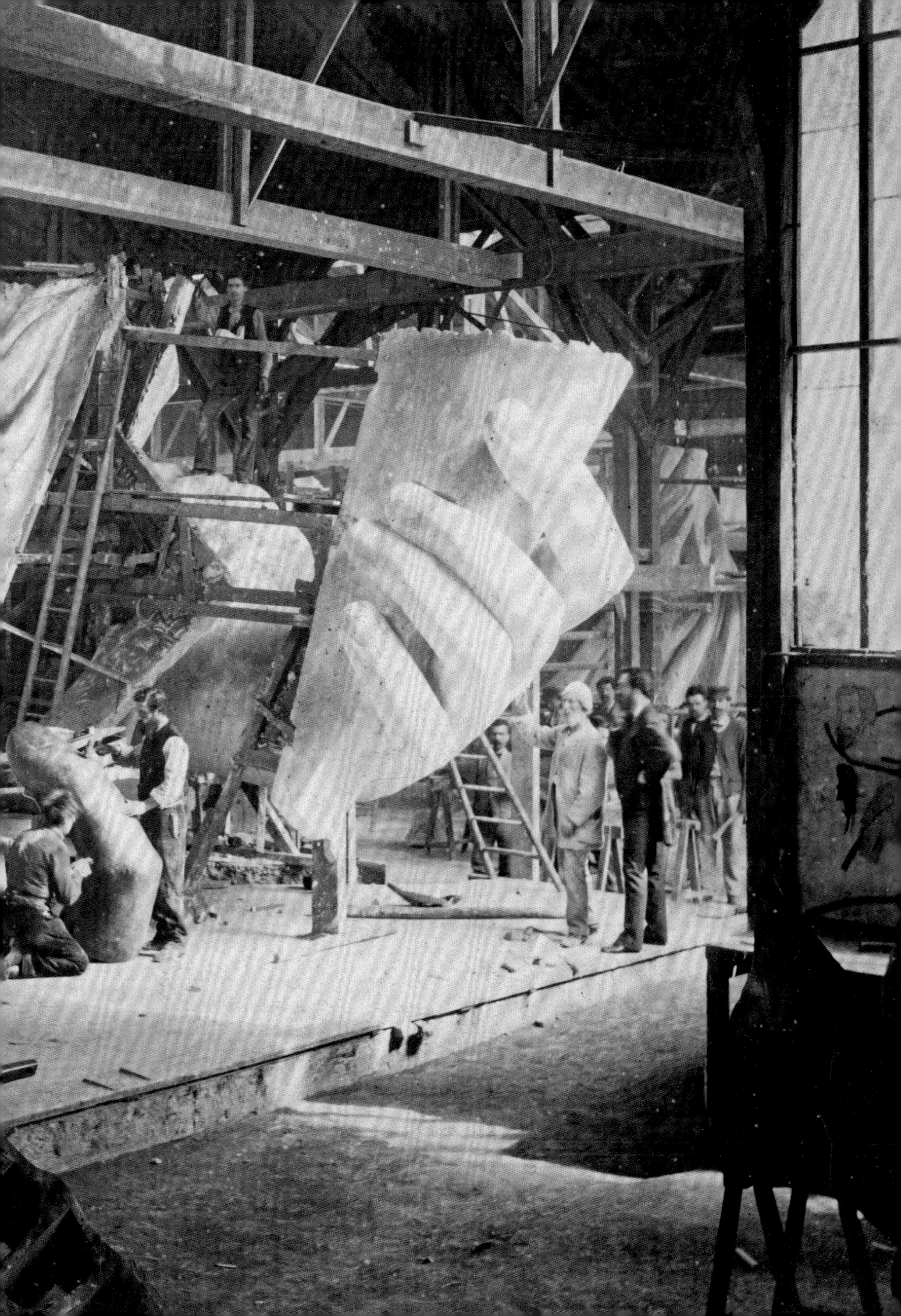

Pierre Petit, *Gaget, Gauthier & Co. Workshop: Construction of the Statue of Liberty*, Paris, 1881–1884. Albumen print, 7.4" × 10" (18.8 × 25.4 cm). Preparation and hammering of the copper sheets attached to wooden jigs.

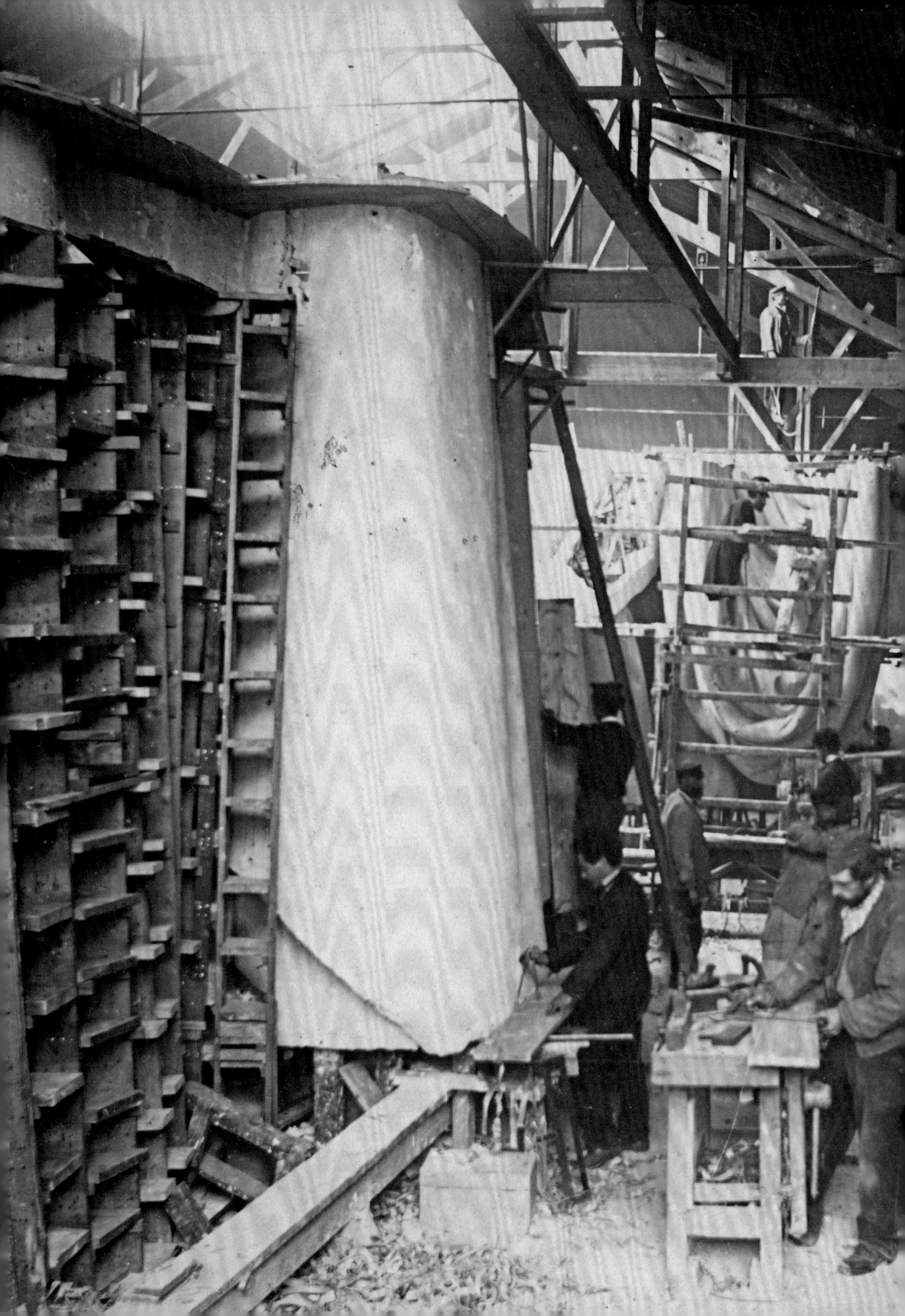

Pierre Petit, *Gaget, Gauthier & Co. Workshop: Construction of the Statue of Liberty*, Paris, 1881–1884. Albumen print, 7.4" × 10" (18.8 × 25.5 cm), on cardboard 11.3" × 13.8" (28.8 × 35 cm).

Pierre Petit, *Gaget, Gauthier & Co. Workshop: Construction of the Statue of Liberty*, Paris, 1881–1884. Albumen print, 7.6" × 10" (19.2 × 25.5 cm), on cardboard, 11.4" × 13.8" (29 × 35 cm).
Once the fine copper plaques that make up the statue's outer layer were completed, the actual sized plaster models were destroyed piece by piece. The same was done to the woodwork used during the statue's construction. The plaster torch was the first to be reduced into pieces in such a manner, followed by the head and so forth, to make room for the preparation of the remaining pieces.

Pierre Petit, *Panoramic View of the Gaget, Gauthier & Co. Workshop*, Paris, 1881. Albumen print, 3.8" × 14.3" (9.7 × 36.2 cm).
This group of three retouched albuminized paper shots create a photomontage of the panoramic view of the 1881 Gaget and Gauthier's workshop. On the right is the where the first of the building's 300,000 rivets would be placed by the American ambassador Morton. At the center, wearing a peaked cap, is Marie Simon, Bartholdi's right hand, foreman and "valiant help," as described by Ferdinand de Lesseps during his July 4, 1884 speech.

The arm holding the torch was the first piece to be completed, in 1876. The statue in its entirety should have been completed by the centennial anniversary of the United States' Declaration of Independence, however, work was delayed and the construction site slowed. With the backing of the Franco-American Union, Bartholdi shipped the torch that same year in 1876 to present it during the Centennial Exposition held in Philadelphia. Measuring 33 feet (10 m) in height, the flame arrived in the city of the Liberty Bell on August 14. It was next brought to Madison Square, where it would stay until 1877 when it was returned to Paris to be placed on the statue, 150 feet (46 m) above ground. While it was in Paris, the torch could be visited by up to 12 people at a time on payment of an entry fee toward the project's execution, and find themselves standing on the balcony that surrounded the flame.

Armed with photographs and mock-ups, Bartholdi used his trip to the United States as the opportunity to name his work the "Statue of American Independence." He also defended his decision to place the colossal beacon on Bedloe's Island. The United States Congress ultimately voted on a joint solution in 1877: the gift of the statue was accepted and the new president was put in charge of deciding its future location, as well as organizing its unveiling ceremony and its maintenance as a "beacon" as well as a "work of art."

Emmanuel Flamant, *The Statue of American Independence, viewed from the Monduit, Gaget, Gauthier & Co. workshop, manufacturers*, Paris, 25 rue de Chazelles, 1889. Albumen print, 10.6" × 8.5" (27 × 21.5 cm). In 1876, 100 years after the United States declared independence, and the year the statue should have been completed, only the torch was finished. The hand holding the torch is photographed here in front of a uniformly colored curtain, a common contrivance in studio portrait photography. The subject was distinguished from a neutral background to make the subject stand out. Hidden from view here is the mess and intense activity of the rue de Chazelles workshop in Paris.

Sharing the Flame

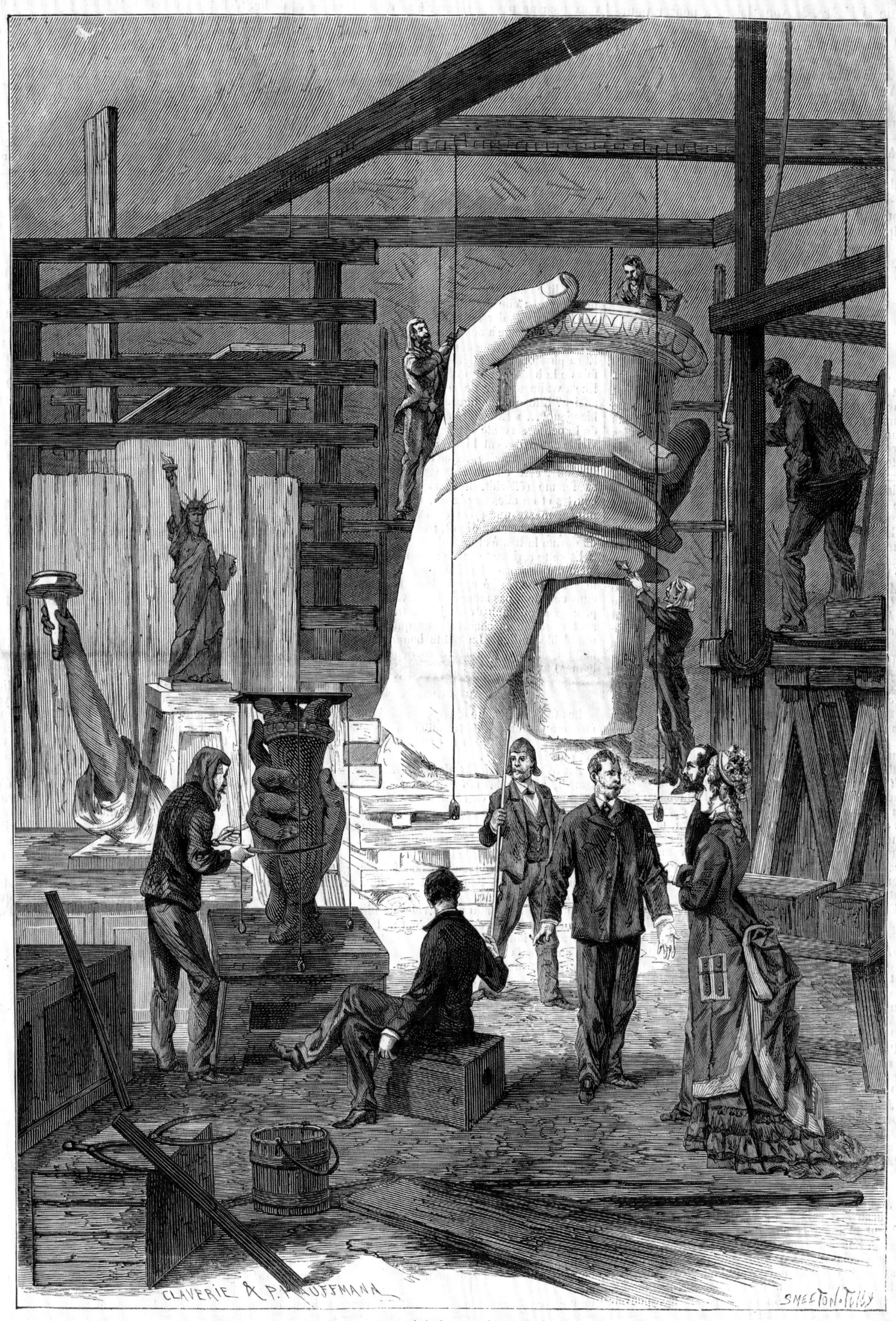

La statue colossale de la Liberté à ériger à l'entrée du port de New-York.

ATELIER DE M. BARTHOLDI OU S'EXÉCUTENT LES DIFFÉRENTES PARTIES DE LA STATUE.

BELOW

Unknown artist, *The 100th Anniversary of the Independence of the United States*, in *Le Monde illustré*, October 9, 1875. Printed engraving.
Having crossed the Atlantic, the torch arrived in Philadelphia and its installation at the Centennial Exposition site could begin.

OPPOSITE

Burn Smeeton, based on the Claverie and Kauffmann drawing, *The Colossal Statue of Liberty at the New York Port Entrance: Mr. Bartholdi's Workshop Where the Statue's Different Parts were Manufactured*, in *L'Illustration*, 34th year, Vol. 67, No. 1733, May 13, 1876, p. 312. Printed engraving, 12.2" × 8.7" (31 × 22 cm).

The plaster statue model that was used to build the final copper plaques was being finished at the Gaget and Gauthier workshops. Models of parts assisted in creating wooden jigs, which were in turn used as guides for hammering the copper plaques that formed the statue. This giant plaster model was 16 times larger than the original model, which measured approximately 4 feet (1.25 m) and is seen here in the far left of the photograph.

Edward L. Wilson and W. Irving Adams, *The Torch on Display During the Philadelphia Centennial Exposition*, 1876. Albumen print, 3.9" × 3.1" (9.8 × 7.8 cm).

"The large arm is outstretched and I would say, without any modesty, that this is a very beautiful and striking piece," Bartholdi wrote to his mother in 1876. During the Philadelphia Exposition, the torch's base was transformed into a souvenir shop. Stereoscopic images of the land surrounding the statue were sold, as well as copies of Wilson and Adams' photographs.

Liberty was further appropriated through the public visits to the torch, including its copper balcony and the view it offered. The French sculptor's "genius" and "skill" were lauded by the press, despite the occasional negative comment, such as that which appeared in the *New York Times* on September 29, 1876, published after the Philadelphia Exposition. It mocked the concept behind the French gift, stating that "it would unquestionably be in poor taste to criticize a statue that you receive as a gift but [...] when a nation promises to another a colossal-sized bronze woman and, after having given you an arm, quietly lets the recipient know that this fragment is actually the only gift since the rest of the woman is to be purchased at the latter's expense, there is a disproportionality between the promise and its fulfillment — one that can be forgiven, but not ignored."

OPPOSITE

The Hand of the Statue of Liberty Displayed at the Philadelphia Exposition, in *Frank Leslie's Illustrated Newspaper. Historical Register of the Centennial Exposition*, 1876, p. 239. Printed engraving, 5.7" × 4.5" (14.6 × 11.5 cm) excluding margins.

OPPOSITE

Edward L. Wilson and W. Irving Adams, *The Torch on Display During the Philadelphia Centennial Exposition*, 1876. Albumen print, 10" × 8.2" (25.5 × 20.9 cm), on cardboard, 17.7" × 15" (45 × 38 cm).

The statue's arm was nevertheless enthusiastically welcomed, to the point where the city thought about adopting it for its own: "Philadelphia," wrote Bartholdi, "has entertained [...] the thought of accepting the monument for its own. Based on their patriotism, they deserve it [...] But I reminded myself of the idea of placing it on land that belongs to all the United States' citizens that also is the most visible, at the entrance to this great American country." (Quoted in Janet Headley's "Bartholdi's Second Trip to the United States: The Philadelphia Exposition [1876]," in *The Statue of Liberty, the Centennial Exposition*, Musée des Arts Décoratifs / Selections from the Reader's Digest.)

STATUE of LIBERTY
2025-COLOSSAL HAND AND TORCH "LIBERTY."

John J. Garnett, *Putting Arm in Position at Madison Square, in Frank Leslie's Illustrated Newspaper*, New York, B.W. Dinsmore and Co., 1886, p. 41. Printed engraving, 5.5" × 4.3" (14 × 11 cm) excluding margins. Following their display in Philadelphia, Liberty's torch and hand were sent to New York to be installed in Madison Square. The transportation and installation of these two components were recorded and disseminated by the press.

OPPOSITE

Anonymous, *The Torch Exhibited in Madison Square*, New York, 1876. Albumen print, 8.2" × 5.7" (20.8 × 14.4 cm). The torch's installation in Madison Square incited some journalists to mock the outstretched hand that seemed to be begging and was sent in place of the statue itself. Such was the case in a *New York Times* editorial in 1876: "Although the arm's arrival would signal a proof that the rest of the statue should follow shortly, there have been some who seriously question this [...]. If the French sculptor had really envisioned a complete statue of Liberty, he would have began with the foundations, then sculpted the shoes, the stockings, and finally the entire legs clad in the stockings."

Unknown author, *The Arm of Bartholdi's Colossal Statue of Liberty in Madison Square, New York,* in *The Daily Graphic*, No. 1250, March 20, 1877, p. 133. Printed engraving, 5.6" × 6.8" (14.3 × 17.3 cm).

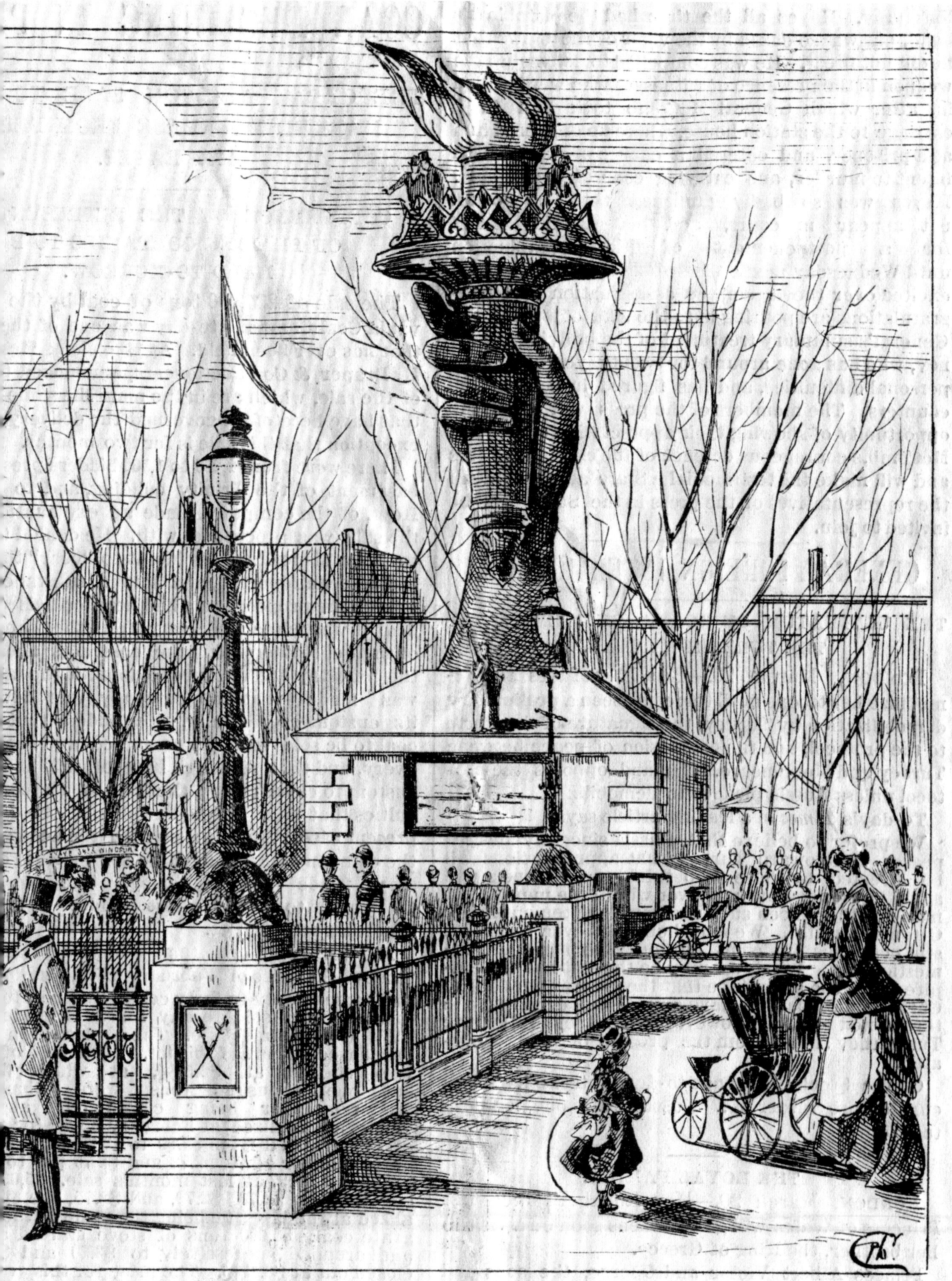

RTHOLDI'S COLOSSAL STATUE OF LIBERTY

ON A TEMPORARY PEDESTAL IN MADISON SQUARE.

OPPOSITE

Auguste Tilly, *Birds Attracted to the Light of the Torch*, in *L'Illustration*, October 29, 1887. Printed engraving.
A year after the Statue of Liberty's inauguration in New York Bay, the damage caused by its electric torch — which was not environmentally friendly from the start — is denounced by the press. The article accompanying this fantasy-riddled engraving was filled with environmental concerns: "We know that the torch held by the Statue of Liberty situated on Bedloe's Island, before New York, is an electric torch of incredible power. Thousands of birds are colliding with the magnifying lenses and circling them like clouds, all attracted to the light. This inconvenience was anticipated, as it is the same for all beacons, but it was never imagined to be so serious. The bird migration to South America is only beginning, but the torch's light is so fascinating that they are already coming to kill themselves en masse, as is demonstrated by the engraving made of this curious event. The majority are injuring their heads, while others fall onto the rail, fatally wounded. In a morning, a total of 13,450 birds were picked up, all of various species!"

Unknown author, *The Statue of Liberty in New York*, in *L'Illustration*, July 4, 1885. Printed engraving.
The engraving projecting the Statue of Liberty's flame on its future site in New York was published on *L'Illustration*'s first page. As the accompanying text states, the engraving came from the American journal *Frank Leslie's Illustrated Newspaper*. It gave "the idea of the splendid panorama that the spectator will be treated to once he or she climbs the steps that are built inside the statue. Once the spectator reaches the balcony that forms the torch's base, held in the statue's hand, the viewer would have the impression of dominating over the port and the city from a hundred meters high". The journalist also reminded the reader that *L'Illustration* had previously announced "the departure of the giant statue of Liberty *Enlightening the World* to America, a gift from France to the United States that is meant to be placed on one of the islets located at the entrance of the New York Bay. Mr. Bartholdi's work has received an enthusiastic welcome from the other side of the Atlantic; the work on the installation is being pushed forward with great gusto. The American newspapers are filled with information on the subject". Liberty's transatlantic adventure resembled a suspense series where the illustrated story line was brimming with anticipatory images.

LE FLAMBEAU ÉLECTRIQUE DE LA STATUE DE « LA LIBERTÉ »

A NEW-YORK

Creating the statue's face and rendering its timeless expression was a serious challenge. Bartholdi, knowing the large distances from which it would be seen, accentuated its features: the arch of the brows was pronounced, the eye sockets were carved out and the nose was flattened.

Skill was necessary with the copper hammering to depict the brows' furrow, the pout and Lady Liberty's controlled and somber look.

As was the case with the torch that was completed in 1876, the head was finished and then exhibited in 1878, this time close to the Champ-de-Mars in Paris, on the Exposition Universelle site. Bartholdi dreamed of placing the giant head at the entrance of the new Palace of Industry, a "coliseum of iron and glass" built by, among others, Gustave Eiffel.

Although it was finally installed on the Champ-de-Mars esplanade, the head proved to be just as great an attraction during the exposition. Visitors could climb the spiral wooden staircase up to the skull dome and the diadem and take in the beautiful Parisian view.

Located at the base, the Franco-American Union stand sold souvenirs: blue satin badges embroidered with the sculpture's motif, printed scarves and miniatures of the bronze head.

Auguste Bartholdi, *Installation of the Ultimately Chosen Head of the Statue of Liberty Enlightening the World, During the 1878 Exposition Universelle in Paris*, 1877. Gouache and cutout, 3" × 2.2" (7.5 × 5.5 cm), pasted on a lithograph by Muller from a drawing by H. Scott depicting the title page of the newspaper *Le Monde illustré* from October 7 , 1877, 15" × 10.6" (38 × 27 cm).
Auguste Bartholdi wanted the statue's copper head to be displayed in a strategic location during the 1878 Exposition Universelle — at the entrance to the famous Palace of Industry, designed by Léopold Hardy, Henri de Dion and Gustave Eiffel. This palace was meant to house both a gallery filled with machines and rooms that displayed paintings in a traditional manner . Bartholdi's ambition was curbed, however, by the Exposition's commissioners, who decided to display the head near the palace of iron and glass, on Champ-de-Mars.

Liberty in Mind

LE MONDE ILLUSTRÉ

JOURNAL HEBDOMADAIRE

ABONNEMENTS POUR PARIS ET LES DÉPARTEMENTS
Un an, 24 fr.; — Six mois, 13 fr.; — Trois mois, 7 fr.; — Un numéro, 50 c.
Le volume semestriel, 12 fr. broché. — 17 fr., relié et doré sur tranche.
LA COLLECTION DES 20 ANNÉES FORME 40 VOLUMES.
Directeur, M. PAUL DALLOZ.

BUREAUX
13, QUAI VOLTAIRE
21e Année. N° 1069 — 7 Oct. 1877

DIRECTION ET ADMINISTRATION, 13, QUAI VOLTAIRE
Toute demande d'abonnement non accompagnée d'un bon sur Paris ou sur la poste, toute demande de numéro à laquelle ne sera pas joint le montant en timbres-poste, seront considérées comme non avenues. — On ne répond pas des manuscrits envoyés.
Administrateur, M. BOURDILLIAT. — *Secrétaire*, M. E. HUBERT.

NE PAS COUPER CE NUMÉRO AVANT DE L'OUVRIR

EXPOSITION UNIVERSELLE DE 1878. — Entrée principale du Palais du Champ-de-Mars. — (Dessin de M. Scott.)

Anonymous, attributed to Charles Marville. *Gaget, Gauthier & Co. Workshop: Building the Statue of Liberty, the Head*, Paris, 1876–1878. Albumen print, 12.4" × 10" (31.5 × 25.5 cm).
This snapshot was probably used to prepare a reproduction or engraving of the print, and has been retouched to specify which areas were to be highlighted.

Pierre Petit, based on a Charles Marville photograph, *Gaget, Gauthier & Co. Workshop: Building the Statue of Liberty, the Head*, Paris, 1881–1884. Albumen print, 7.7" × 5.2" (19.6 × 13.1 cm).
Here, Pierre Petit and his patron, Bartholdi, have emphasized Liberty's head by enhancing several parts of the image in brown and white, in order to highlight the contrasts.

Auguste Trichon, based on a Pierre Petit photograph, in *L'Univers illustré*, 21st year, No. 1189, January 5, 1878, p. 8. Printed engraving, 12.2" × 9" (31 × 22.8 cm).
The fascination surrounding the Liberty worksite constantly prompted questions about the statue's scale, measurements and excessiveness. On the several levels of scaffolding, plasterers shaped the giant face, while the public visited the site.

TRAVAUX DU MONUMENT COMMÉMORATIF DE L'INDÉPENDANCE DES ÉTATS-UNIS, DANS L'ATELIER DE M. BARTHOLDI.

Voir la Chronique.

Claverie, *Casting the Statue's Head in the Monduit and Béchet Workshop, in L'Illustration*, No. 1819, January 5, 1878. Printed engraving, 12.3" × 8.7" (31.2 × 22.1 cm) excluding margins. Models of the statue and its components decorated the workshop, and were used during the manufacture of the plasters, which resulted from an enlargement of 1/16 of the models.

LA STATUE COLOSSALE DE LA LIBERTÉ, DESTINÉE A L'ENTRÉE DU PORT DE NEW-YORK.
MODELAGE DE LA TÊTE DE LA STATUE DANS LES ATELIERS DE MM. MONDUIT ET BECHEER, A PARIS.

Auguste Bartholdi, *Installation of the Final Copper Head of the Statue of Liberty During the 1878 Exposition Universelle in Paris,* circa 1877. Gouached paper cutout on albumen paper, mounted on cardboard, 13.3" × 21" (33.8 × 53.4 cm). This large-scale composition reproduced the form of the Statue of Liberty head through the use of photographic imaging on albumen. It was similar to Bartholdi's original photographic panorama of New York that he used earlier in Paris. Bartholdi retouched, cut out and glued his head installation projects during the Exposition Universelle.

FOLLOWING PAGES

Anonymous, *Head of the Statue of Liberty Exhibited in Paris,* circa 1875. Albumen print, 4" × 2.7" (10.2 × 6.9 cm). Charles Marville, *Public Exhibition of the Head of the Statue of Liberty*, Paris, circa 1878. Albumen print, 14.6" × 10" (37.2 × 25.1 cm). After displays of the hand and torch in Philadelphia and New York, the statue then showed its head in Paris on the Champ-de-Mars: "Seen from the Exposition's Belgian restaurant, the Statue has an expression of severe firmness that is not apparent when close by." (*La France*, October 17, 1878.)

5
10
15
20
25

Unknown author, *The Head of the Statue of Liberty at the Paris Exposition Universelle, 1878*, in *L'Univers illustré*, No. 1227, September 28, 1878. Printed engraving, 12.2" × 8.9" (31 × 22.7 cm) excluding margins. The torch and the head were made accessible thanks to the forty or so cast iron (and some wooden) steps that offered access to a view later extolled by English writer Rudyard Kipling.

616 L'UNIVERS ILLUSTRÉ

EXPOSITION UNIVERSELLE. — TÊTE DE LA STATUE DE LA LIBERTÉ, œuvre de M. Bartholdi.

La statue colossale de *la Liberté éclairant le monde* doit être érigée sur un îlot à l'entrée du port de New-York, où elle servira de phare. — Voir page 618.

RIGHT PAGE

Unknown author, *The Head of the Statue of Liberty* in Paris, on mounting board, "Franco-American Union, souvenir of the 100th anniversary of the independence of the United States, 1776–1876," 1878. Albumen print, 7.7" × 5.2" (19.6 × 13.3 cm), on cardboard, 14.3" × 9.8" (36.4 × 25 cm). Although paid shows were prohibited at the Exposition Universelle, the committee bypassed this restriction by regulating access to the top of the head. Those who had bought a photograph from the committee or who had paid for a visit to the diorama were given permission to enter. Souvenirs bearing the statue's image were also available for purchase.

FOLLOWING PAGES

Henri Saintin, *The Head of the Statue of Liberty Displayed at Champ-de-Mars, Exposition Universelle*, Paris, 1878. Oil on panel, 5.9" × 9.1" (15 × 23 cm).

ŒUVRE NATIONALE de L'UNION FRANCO-AMERICAINE
MONUMENT de L'INDEPENDANCE
LA LIBERTE ECLAIRANT le MONDE
PAR Aug BARTHOLDI Statuaire
PAR MONDUIT GAGET GAUTHIER

Henri Saintin

Eugène Viollet-le-Duc died in 1879. Bartholdi then turned to Gustave Eiffel, the famous engineer renowned for his artistic iron works, who would hire another talented engineer, Maurice Koechlin, to develop a new framework that would support Liberty's exterior. Stepping away from Viollet-le-Duc's technical solutions, Koechlin decided to use a lightweight and metal frame made entirely of iron, to which the copper plaques forming the skin of the statue would be affixed. Construction of this full-scale frame began on October 24, 1881, but the building of the complete model structure required two years and eight months of work.

Measuring approximately 150 feet (46 m) in height and weighing 220 tons (200 tonnes) — 132 tons (120 tonnes) of which belonged to the frame, and the outer layer a full 88 tons (80 tonnes) — Liberty Enlightening the World overlooked the Plaine Monceau rooftops. Parisians had become accustomed to it, and visitors to the workshop — the most famous being Victor Hugo who visited on November 24, 1884 — took pleasure in making the climb to the head.

On July 4, 1884, the celebration day of America's independence, Ferdinand de Lesseps, the new president of the Franco-American Union, signed, along with Auguste Bartholdi, the deed gifting the statue to the United States. The sculptor immortalized the moment by proudly posing at the foot of his giant creation.

Pierre Petit, *Gaget, Gauthier & Co. workshop, building the Statue of Liberty, Levi P. Morton installing the first rivet*, Paris, 1881. Albumen print, 6.7" × 4.8" (17 × 12.2 cm).
The construction of the base and the scaffolding that would hold the statue as it was being completed began on Monday, October 24, 1881, at 3 p.m. at the plumbing and copper smelting workshops on rue de Chazelles, in the 17th arrondissement in Paris. The ceremony's guest of honor was the new ambassador to the United States, Levi Parsons Morton. The event was covered extensively by the press, thanks to the reproduction of engravings of several photographs taken during the occasion. The crowd assembled around the copper foot, on which the giant's toes could be clearly distinguished, while Gustave Eiffel's metallic structure emerged a few meters above the ground. The background shows buildings under construction, as Paris was being transformed under the guidance of the prefect of the Seine, Georges-Eugène Haussmann. These buildings would be completed at the same time as the statue's test model. In the meantime the real show, construction in the open air, had begun.

A Parisian Construction

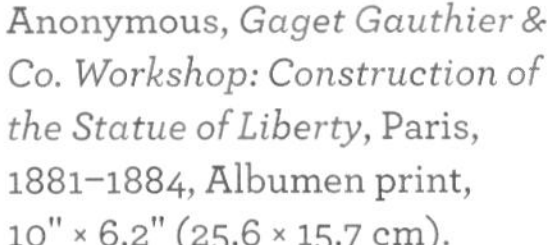

Anonymous, *Gaget Gauthier & Co. Workshop: Construction of the Statue of Liberty*, Paris, 1881–1884, Albumen print, 10" × 6.2" (25.6 × 15.7 cm).

Albert Fernique, *Gaget, Gauthier & Co. Workshop: Construction of the Statue of Liberty*, Paris, 1881–1884. Albumen print, 17.3" × 10.7" (44 × 27.2 cm).

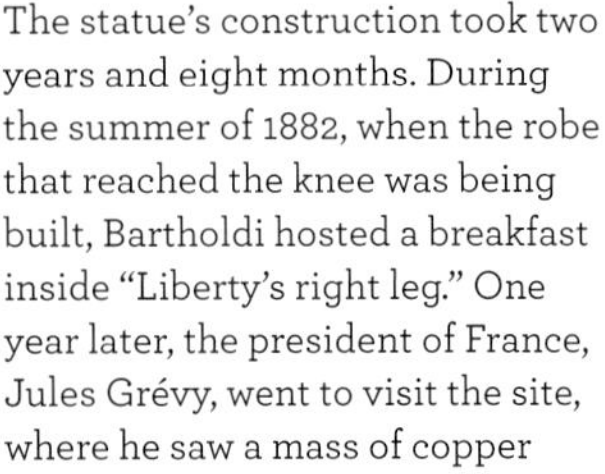

The statue's construction took two years and eight months. During the summer of 1882, when the robe that reached the knee was being built, Bartholdi hosted a breakfast inside "Liberty's right leg." One year later, the president of France, Jules Grévy, went to visit the site, where he saw a mass of copper from which an iron pylon jutted out in lieu of an arm. During this occasion, he was invited to undertake an unusual climb that started at the statue's right foot, which had a gaping sole. "The iron framing, which is the copper exterior's fulcrum, creates a kind of large pylon which has four points attached to the stonework base that supports the statue. Each of these points will be supported by three foundation bolts of 0.140 m [5½ inches] in diameter, sealed 15 meters [50 feet] deep." (*Le Génie civil*, 1883.)

Attributed to Pierre Petit, *Gaget, Gauthier & Co. Workshop: Building the Statue of Liberty*, Paris, 1881–1884. Albumen print, 10.1" × 7.7" (25.7 × 19.6 cm).

Pierre Petit, *Gaget, Gauthier & Co. Workshop: Building the Statue of Liberty*, Paris, 1881–1884. Albumen print, 10" × 7.4" (25.5 × 18.8 cm) (unmounted proofs).

Albert Fernique, *Gaget, Gauthier & Co. Workshop: Building the Statue of Liberty*, Paris, 1884. Albumen print, 18.2" × 13.1" (46.2 × 33.4 cm).
In the spring of 1884, the statue, still flanked by its scaffolding, was almost complete. In the background, Haussmann's buildings were also being finalized.

Victor Dargaud, *The Statue of Liberty in the Gaget, Gauthier & Co. Workshop, rue de Charelles*, 1884. Oil on canvas, 12.6" × 18.1" (32 × 46 cm).

FOLLOWING PAGES

Narcisse Navellier and Alexandre Léon Marie, from Pierre Petit's photographs, *Documents on the Work of the Franco-American Union*, 1883. Engraving.
Several highlights from the Statue of Liberty's Parisian construction were reproduced through engravings, which were themselves created from drawings based on photographs. Shown at the bottom, the raised right foot was left hollow, allowing people the chance to squeeze themselves inside the colossus. Shown in the center, the body covered in scaffolds that allow the iron colonnade to escape (it would later become the statue's raised arm). To its right and to its left, two sectional images show the iron frame of the statue, which would become its skeleton.

Claverie, engraved by Auguste Tilly, from a photograph by Eugène Chéron, *L'Illustration*, 42nd year, Vol. 83, No. 2145, April 5, 1884, p. 216. Drawing, 12.2" × 8.5" (31 × 21.5 cm).
The sight of the giant statue looming over the roofs and filling the Paris sky garnered a renewed interest in the spectacle. In this image, the engraver has highlighted the sky covered in clouds and chimney smoke, unstable and variable shapes contrasting with the copper giant's monumental immobility.

Le
Petit Journal
7000000
5
Dargaud

Les travaux de la statue colossale de la Liberté

Par Aug. BARTHOLDI

Exécutée aux Ateliers Gaget, Gauthier et Cie, 25, rue de Chazelles (Parc Monceau)

1. Construction en bois de la main gauche de la statue. — 2. Modelage du même fragment, revêtu de plâtre. — 3. Coupe de la construction intérieure de la statue (vue de face). — 4. Érection de la statue dans la cour de l'usine. 5. Coupe (vue de profil). — 6. Moulage en bois d'un fragment au moyen de formes prises par les menuisiers.
7. Battage du cuivre dans les formes exécutées par les menuisiers. — 8. Visite de M. le Président de la République dans l'intérieur de la statue. Entrée par le pied droit.

LA STATUE-PHARE DE LA « LIBERTÉ », DESTINÉE A LA VILLE DE NEW-YORK
D'après une photographie de M. Chéron.

Attributed to Émile Bayard, *Presentation to Mr. Morton, Minister of the United States, of the Statue of Liberty by Auguste Bartholdi*, 1884. Graphite pencil, ink, wash and white gouache on cardboard, 17.7" × 12.3" (44.9 × 31.2 cm).
July 4, 1884, the date of the national American holiday, was also the day the statue was presented to the United States. The head and the arm brandishing the torch were freed from their scaffolding constraints: "The American and French colors flutter in the wind up to the torch's platform." Accompanied by the American anthem, which was interpreted by the Batignolles orchestra, Ambassador Morton, on behalf on the American president, accepted the gift of the colossal statue of *Liberty Enlightening the World*. This was the first time the public could climb the statue up to the diadem.

OPPOSITE

Albert Bellenger, from a drawing attributed to Émile Bayard, *Delivery of the Statue of Liberty to Mr. Morton, United States Ambassador, on July 4, 1884*, in *L'Illustration*, July 12, 1884, p. 32. Hand-colored engraving, 12.2" × 8.7" (31 × 22 cm) excluding margins, on page, 15.1" × 10.8" (38.3 × 27.5 cm).
In this engraving, the sky, filled with the statue born from its scaffolding, is alternately colored red and blue: the colors of the French and American flags. The French gift to America is finally checked over and readied for its dismantling to be safely transported.

PARIS. — REMISE A M. MORTON, MINISTRE DES ÉTATS-UNIS, DE LA STATUE DE LA « LIBERTÉ », PAR M. BARTHOLDI

Remise de la statue colossale de la LIBERTÉ à M. Morton, ambassadeur des États-Unis.

Dessin de Henri MEYER. — Voir l'article, page 219.

Drawing by Henri Meyer, *Delivery of the Statue of Liberty to Mr. Morton, United States Ambassador, on July 4, 1884,* in *Le Journal illustré*, July 13, 1884. Printed engraving, 12.4" × 8.5" (31.5 × 21.5 cm) excluding margins, on page, 15.5" × 11.6" (39.3 × 29.5 cm).

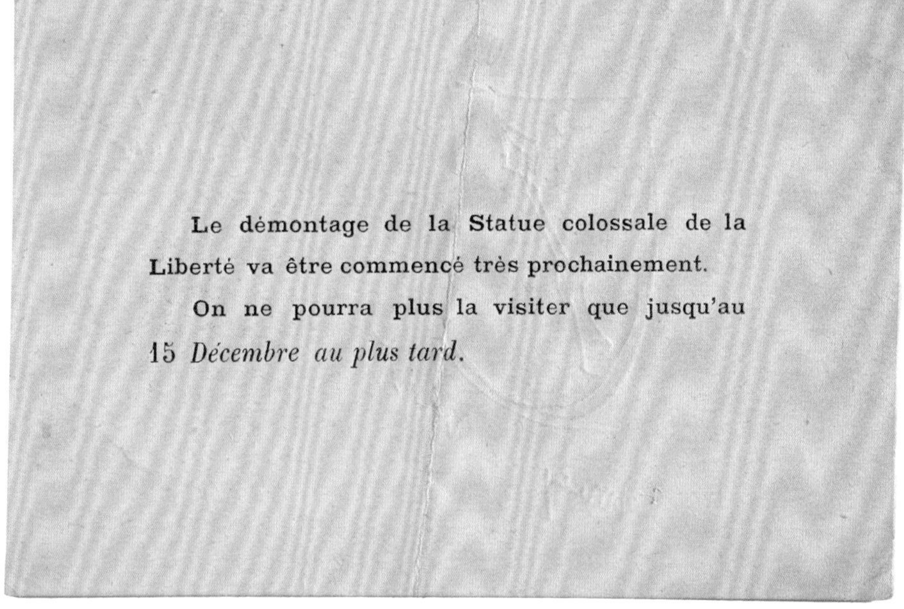

Le démontage de la Statue colossale de la Liberté va être commencé très prochainement.

On ne pourra plus la visiter que jusqu'au 15 *Décembre au plus tard.*

The dismantling of the colossal Statue of Liberty will be begun very soon.

We can only visit it until December 15 at the latest.

Unknown author, *Completion of Construction of the Statue of Liberty in Paris,* 1884. Printed vignette, 2.8" × 4.2" (7 × 10.7 cm).

By the end of 1875, Bartholdi rendered his first model that was first started in 1871. In the statue's left hand he placed a tablet, on which was inscribed "July IV MDCCLXXVI," the date of the declaration of independence that marked America's political liberation. On April 25, 1876, Laboulaye placed the project of the "American liberty" on the side of "truth, justice, light and the law." Even the statue's material, of "virgin copper," was described as the "fruit of labor and peace." Financing the statue's construction was a considerable feat. Created in 1874, the Franco-American Union deployed, together with Bartholdi, a whole arsenal of means and innovative solutions to raise money. A subscription was launched, followed by dinners, banquets, parties, lotteries, raffles, various statue-themed products and miniatures, performances ranging from opera to diorama, not to mention visits to the construction sites and the expositions featuring the torch and the head.

Edward Windsor Kemble, *The Statue of Liberty as It Will Appear by the Time the Pedestal is Finished*, in *Life*, January 17, 1884. Printed engraving.
In 1884, due to lack of funds, the future of the American pedestal of the Statue of Liberty was still not secured. This cover of *Life* turned the situation into one of ridicule, depicting Lady Liberty as decrepit and exhausted after waiting so long for her famous base.

The Price of Liberty

VOLUME III. NEW YORK, JANUARY 17, 1884. NUMBER 55.
Entered at New York Post Office as Second-Class Mail Matter.

THE STATUE OF LIBERTY
AS IT WILL APPEAR BY THE TIME THE PEDESTAL IS FINISHED.

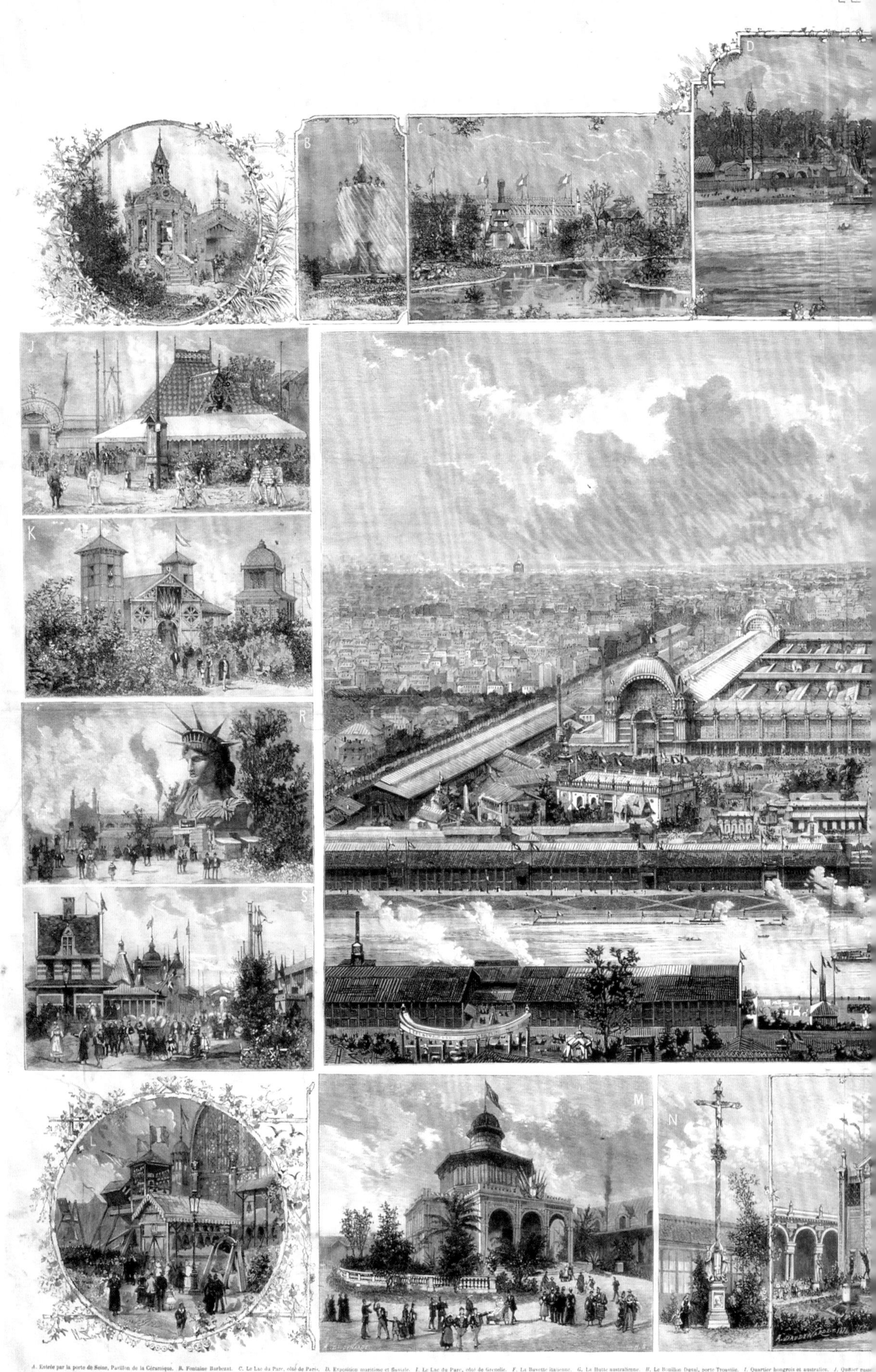
LE
A. Entrée par la porte de Seine, Pavillon de la Céramique. B. Fontaine Barbezat. C. Le Lac du Parc, côté de Paris. D. Exposition maritime et fluviale. E. Le Lac du Parc, côté de Grenelle. F. La Buvette italienne. G. La Hutte australienne. H. Le Bouillon Duval, porte Trouville. I. Quartier hongrois et australien. J. Quartier russ
LE VRAI PANORAMA D
Dessins de M. Scott.

USTRÉ
C
H
I
T
U
O
P
Q
V
DUVAL
M. Pavillon de Monaco. N. Calvaire de M. Le Goffe. O. Pavillon de la Ville de Paris. P. La Façade de la Gare du Champ-de-Mars. Q. Le Pavillon des Travaux publics. R. La Tête de la Statue de la Liberté. S. Quartier hollandais, danois et belge. T. Pavillon espagnol. U. Pavillon de la Photochromie et de la Photoglyptie. V. La Czarda.
MARS AVEC SES ANNEXES
Supplément du n° 1126 du Monde illustré.

PREVIOUS PAGES

Scott and various engravers, *1878 Exposition Universelle in Paris*, in *Le Monde illustré*, No. 1126, October 26, 1878, supplement. Engraving plank, canvas folder, 27.4" × 37.8" (69.5 × 96 cm).
The age of the Statue of Liberty was also the golden age for the Expositions Universelles. As recent as the arrival of photographs in newspapers, these displays created a real competition between nations who were rivals and would present their industrial and architectural innovations. At the intersection of art, architecture and industry, the head of the statue presented at the 1876 Exposition was a spectacular achievement.

Pierre Petit, *Model of the Statue of Liberty Enlightening the World*, Galerie Contemporaine plank (new series, series I, 1884–1885, No. 75). Photoglypty (Goupil & Co.), 9.8" × 7.6" (25 × 19.2 cm), pasted on cardboard, 13.5" × 10.1" (34.3 × 25.6 cm).
The Parisian photographer Pierre Petit, a friend of Bartholdi's, reproduced the drawings, watercolors and this Statue of the Liberty model. The photoglypty that was created by Goupil for the Galeries Contemporaines' edition was authorized to produce and sell a large number of these images. It is most likely that Bartholdi got to know this publisher thanks to his childhood friend, the painter Jean-Léon Gérôme, who was Goupil's son-in-law and established his workshop at the same address.

PALAIS DE L'INDUSTRIE
CHAMPS-ÉLYSÉES
UNION FRANCO AMÉRICAINE
1776
1876
DIORAMA
représentant
LE MONUMENT COMMÉMORATIF DE L'INDÉPENDANCE
DES
ÉTATS-UNIS D'AMÉRIQUE
&
LA VILLE & RADE DE NEW-YORK
ENTRÉE 1fr de 10H. à 6 heures

DIORAMA
au
JARDIN DES TUILERIES
PRÈS LE GRAND BASSIN
Entrée 1fr.
Dimanches & Fêtes 50c.
4th
JULY
1776
Imp. J. CHÉRET & Cie 18, R. BRUNEL, PARIS
ŒUVRE NATIONALE DE L'UNION FRANCO AMÉRICAINE
VUE DE LA RADE DE NEW-YORK
& DU MONUMENT COMMÉMORATIF DE L'AMITIÉ DE LA FRANCE & DES ÉTATS-UNIS

PREVIOUS PAGES

Unknown author, *Diorama of the Tuileries Garden*, printed by J. Chéret & Co., 18 rue Brunel, Paris, 1878. Colored engraving, vignette, 5.2" × 3.5" (13.3 × 8.9 cm).

Unknown author, *Diorama of the Statue of Liberty*, 1877. Chromolithography, canvas poster, 45.7" × 30.7" (116 × 78 cm).
As it was in vogue in the 1870s, the spectacle of diorama-style shows easily attracted the attention of the French Committee of the Franco-American Union, which, under Bartholdi's supervision, built one in honor of the project "The Statue of Liberty Enlightening the World." The diorama was first installed at the Champs-Élysées inside the Palace of Industry, but was later moved to the Tuileries Garden, and dismantled in 1879. The show used lights and illusions, and placed the spectator as if he or she were standing at the back of a ship leaving New York, discovering the Statue of Liberty bit by bit thanks to a bird's-eye view of the New York Bay. The success of this animation attracted large crowds, and the funds raised from the sale of entrance tickets contributed to the financing of the real, metal statue.

Front page of Joseph Pulitzer's newspaper, *The World,* commending the raising of $100,000 dollars for the construction of the Statue of Liberty's pedestal, August 11, 1885.
One hundred thousand dollars! This was the triumphant conclusion to the *World* fundraising campaign for the pedestal of the Statue of Liberty, in *New York World*, August 11, 1885. Joseph Pulitzer bought the newspaper *New York World* in 1883. A democrat, he was rather removed from the Committee's social and political milieu, but he engaged with them because of his idealism in his search for funds for the construction of the pedestal, in order to embrace the Liberty cause. His memorable call to the people appeared in his editorial on March 16, 1885; "We have to find money at all costs! The *World* is the people's paper and today is calling to each and every one of you... The Statue... it is the laborers, the artisans, the merchants, the vendors who, regardless of their class and their condition, have given the necessary funds. We should show ourselves as being equally up to the challenge. Do not wait on the millionaires of our country to foot the bill." This same zeal would equally characterize the subscription, a chance for the poor to surpass the rich in their contribution to a greater cause. Citizens were encouraged to campaign and the newspaper involved them by regularly publishing the names of those who donated, as well as touching letters written by young children, retirees or immigrants. Pulitzer thus popularized an elitist practice; that of publishing the names of subscribers. Eventually, the editorial writer abandoned the urgent tone used during the fundraising. Rather than focusing on the lack of money, he highlighted instead the donation results. This "sensational" approach worked, especially since the competition between newspapers was growing. The Committee's treasury sped up the cadence to reach the same tempo as the newspaper's print run. These two results — the Committee's earnings and the newspaper's print run — would soon appear on the newspaper's front page, which also integrated the image of Liberty to its logo.

The Copies of THE WORLD Printed and Sold on Sunday Last Aggregated

230,220.

The Average Circulation of THE SUNDAY WORLD is Larger than that of any other Newspaper Published on the Western Hemisphere.

The 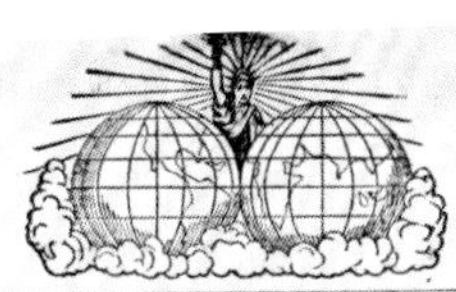 World.

The Copies of THE WORLD Printed and Sold on Sunday Last Aggregated

230,220.

The Average Circulation of THE SUNDAY WORLD is Larger than that of any other Newspaper Published on the Western Hemisphere.

VOL. XXVI., NO. 8,757. NEW YORK, TUESDAY, AUGUST 11, 1885---WITH SUPPLEMENT. PRICE TWO CENTS.

THE SPECTRE IN GRANADA.

A CONDITION MORE HORRIBLE THAN THAT OF NAPLES LAST YEAR.

MURDERED IN HIS HOME.

A WEALTHY BROOKLYNITE SHOT DOWN BY A HIDDEN FOE.

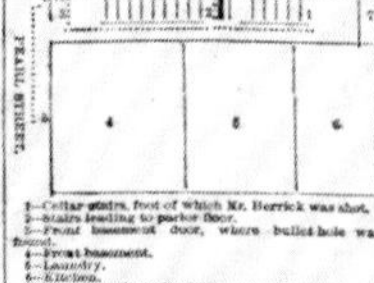

ONE HUNDRED THOUSAND DOLLARS!

TRIUMPHANT COMPLETION OF THE WORLD'S FUND FOR THE LIBERTY PEDESTAL.

Story of the Greatest Popular Subscription Ever Raised in America—How the Republic Was Saved from Lasting Disgrace—An Event for Patriotic Citizens to Rejoice Over—A Roll of Honor Bearing the Names of 120,000 Generous Patriots—The Flags of France and the American Union Floating in Sisterly Sympathy—Over $2,300 Received Yesterday—The Grand Total Foots Up $102,006.39—A Generous Lady Pays $130 for the Washington Cent.

In order to build Liberty in America, it had to be disassembled in Paris and brought across the Atlantic. Piece by piece, the metallic structure was wrapped and placed in over 300 wooden crates that were transported by train from Saint-Lazare station to Rouen. The fragmented statue was then placed on a French navy ship, the *Isère*, destined for New York. The work on the pedestal was still not completed by the festive date of July 4, 1885, despite the excavation for its foundations having started in 1883. Yet the remarkable intervention of journalist Joseph Pulitzer, owner and publisher of *New York World*, on March 6, 1885, electrified the United States and raised the funds necessary to build the giant base conceived by American architect Richard Morris Hunt. The inauguration, under the stewardship of President Cleveland, took place on October 28, 1886, a day that was designated a public holiday so that the population could come and admire the statue. It was a grand occasion, with a large civilian and military parade.

First a Parisian, Liberty became an American before becoming a global citizen.

Henri Thiriat, *The Statue of Liberty in New York: The End of the Assembly*, in *L'Illustration*, 44th year, Vol. 88, No. 2278, October 23, 1886. Printed engraving, 10.1" × 8.6" (25.7 × 21.8 cm).
A giant with copper skin and bones made of iron, Lady Liberty is drawn here a few days before the completion of her reassembly in New York. The copper skin of her face and her raised arm were yet to be finished. Seemingly tiny laborers worked around the giant's neck, some nailing, others pulling or adjusting the metal plates that would envelop her. Published on the first page of *L'Illustration*, this seemingly fantastic drawing fascinated the public. The analogy between this and the giant of *Gulliver's Travels* is evident: "Sitting on a harness suspended by ropes, the laborers have, in comparison to the statue, the proportion of human ants that inevitably invoke thoughts of Lilliputians trying to tie down Gulliver."

New York!

LA STATUE DE LA LIBERTÉ A NEW-YORK. — LA FIN DU MONTAGE

ROUEN. — CHARGEMENT DE LA S

LIBERTÉ », A BORD DE L'« ISÈRE »

PREVIOUS PAGES

Arthur Hauger, *Rouen, Loading the Statue of Liberty onto the* Isère, in *L'Illustration*, June 13, 1885. Printed engraving, 8.5" × 12.4" (21.5 × 31.5 cm) excluding margins. Packed into enormous wooden crates, the dismantled statue took up more than 70 train cars on its ride to Rouen, where it was transferred onto the frigate *Isère*. At the point of departure, on May 21, 1886, Bartholdi and Gaget came aboard the ship. The morning arrival in New York on June 19 was particularly festive, despite the unfinished pedestal, which cast a slight shadow on the event.

Arrival in New York of the Isère, Carrying Mr. Bartholdi's Statue of Liberty, view from the statue's pedestal. Engraving printed in *L'Illustration*, Saturday, July 11, 1885, 43rd year, No. 2211. Announced in the previous *L'Illustration* publication, the statue's arrival in New York was once again presented through images a month later in the same journal. "It was on July 17 that the transport, the *Isère*, anchored at Sandy-Hook after a voyage of 25 days; two days later, it left its anchorage, escorted by four American warships and a fleet of steamboats and vessels carrying thousands of spectators, to stop in front of Bedloe's Island, where the pedestal of the statue stands, to the cheers of an enormous crowd, covered over by the sound of artillery fire from the warships and surrounding forts. Next, the French officers disembarked and made their way to New York's City Hall, in the middle of a procession made up of authorities and militia in full dress uniform playing music."

ARRIVEE A NEW-YORK DE « L'ISÈRE », PORTANT LA STATUE DE « LA LIBERTE », DE M. BARTHOLDI

VUE PRISE DU PIÉDESTAL DE LA STATUE

Unknown author, *The Face of Auguste Bartholdi's Statue of Liberty Before its Vernissage at Bedloe's Island in the Port of New York, Where It Arrived on June 19, 1885*, Photograph.
Wedged between wooden frames, Lady Liberty's face, with a somewhat worried expression, waited patiently for her iron skeleton to be erected and for her copper skin to be affixed. Unpacked from their wooden crates, Liberty's detached pieces were looked over by amused spectators.

Unknown author, *The Statue of Liberty in New York: Assembling the Metallic Structure on the Pedestal*, 1886. Photograph. The work of digging out the pedestal's foundations as conceived by the American architect Morris Hunt began in 1883 on Bedloe's Island, but its progress was stalled due to a lack of funds. The money needed to finish the job would be raised in March 1885 thanks, in large part, to the journalist Joseph Pulitzer, editor of *The World*.

Unknown author, *The Statue of Liberty in New York: Assembling the Metallic Structure on the Pedestal*, 1886. Photograph. With the giant base finished, it is the turn of the iron reinforcement that makes up the copper statue's skeleton to be built.

Frank Leslie's Illustrated Newspaper, Vol. 63, No. L, New York, November 6, 1886. Printed engraving, 10.9" × 8.8" (27.8 × 22.4 cm).
Based on an overhead photograph, this engraving depicts the military and civil procession on Broadway on the 28th of October, 1886, for the inauguration of the Statue of Liberty. Despite the unfavorable weather, the numerous parades, brass bands (100 were counted) and fireworks attracted, with the sound of cannons and sirens, almost one million people. To reach the statue, officials embarked in the Battery, and were quickly joined by hundreds of people grouped on boats, visible in the background of the engraving.

FOLLOWING PAGES

Charles Graham, *The Illumination of the Port of New York During the Inauguration of the Statue of Liberty*, October 28, 1886. Printed engraving.

FRANK LESLIE'S ILLUSTRATED NEWSPAPER

Entered according to Act of Congress, in the year 1886, by Mrs. Frank Leslie, in the Office of the Librarian of Congress at Washington.—Entered at the Post Office, New York, N.Y., as Second-class Matter.

No. 1,624.—Vol. LXIII.] NEW YORK—FOR THE WEEK ENDING NOVEMBER 6, 1886. [Price, 10 Cents. $4.00 Yearly. 13 Weeks, $1.00

NEW YORK CITY.—THE GRAND DEMONSTRATION ON "LIBERTY DAY," OCTOBER 28th.—THE MILITARY AND CIVIC PROCESSION PASSING DOWN LOWER BROADWAY, WITH THE NAVAL PAGEANT IN THE DISTANCE.

From a Sketch by a Staff Artist.—See Page 182.

OPPOSITE

Currier and Ives, *The great Bartholdi statue, Liberty Enlightening the World: The gift of France to the American people,* 1883. Lithography.

Before the assemblage of the Statue of Liberty is finished in the port of New York, Auguste Bartholdi would distribute several anticipatory drawings placing it at its American location. This view would be reproduced in lithography as well as in photolithography but the number of boats and the colors varied from one plank to another. Yet the image of Lady Liberty on her pedestal evoked the preparatory images that Bartholdi created for "Egypt Enlightening Asia," a monumental sculpture that he dreamed of placing at the entrance of the Suez Canal.

PAGES 126–127

The Gift of France to the American People: The Bartholdi Colossal Statue, Liberty Enlightening the World, 1884. Color lithography, 13.2" × 18.5" (33.5 × 47 cm) (image), 19.4" × 25.9" (49.3 × 65.8 cm) (paper).

PAGE 128

Charles Magnus, *New York. Bartholdi "Statue of Liberty," erected on Bedloe's Island, in New York Harbor,* 1885.

PAGES 129-130

Currier and Ives, The Great Bartholdi Statue, Liberty Enlightening the World: The Gift of France to the American People, 1885. Chromolithography, 13.9" × 9.75" (34.5 × 24.7 cm) (image), 17.75" × 13.5" (45.1 × 34.3 cm) (paper).

PAGE 131

Auguste Bartholdi, 1884. Chromolithography, 33.9" × 23.9" (86.2 × 60.9 cm) (paper).

THE GREAT BARTHOLDI STATUE,
LIBERTY ENLIGHTENING THE WORLD.
THE GIFT OF FRANCE TO THE AMERICAN PEOPLE.
TO BE
ERECTED ON BEDLOE'S ISLAND, NEW YORK HARBOR.

OREGON.
WASHINGTON TER.
MONTANA TER.
DAKOTA TER.
MINNESOTA.
IDAHO TER.
WYOMING TER.
NEBRASKA.
IOWA.
MISSOURI.
KANSAS.
COLORADO.
UTAH TER.
NEVADA.
CALIFORNIA.
ARIZONA TER.
NEW MEXICO TER.
INDIAN TER.
ARKANSAS.
TEXAS.
LOUISIANA.
MISSISSIPPI.
ALABAMA.
GEORGIA.
United

WISCONSIN
MICHIGAN.
NEW YORK.
NEW HAMPSHIRE.
MAINE.
MASSACHUSETTS.
RHODE ISLAND.
CONNECTICUT.
NEW JERSEY.
DELAWARE.
MARYLAND.
DIST. OF COLUMBIA.
PENNSYLVANIA.
OHIO.
INDIANA.
TENNESSEE.
SOUTH CAROLINA.
NORTH CAROLINA.
VIRGINIA.
WEST VIRGINIA.
KENTUCKY.
ILLINOIS.

ING CO,

JERSEY CITY. HOBOKEN.

BROOKLYN, LONG ISLAND CITY.

NEW YORK.

BARTHOLDI "STATUE OF LIBERTY," Erected on Bedloe's Island, in New York Harbor.

PUBLISHED BY CURRIER & IVES, 115 NASSAU ST. N.Y. COPYRIGHT 1885 BY CURRIER & IVES, N.Y.

THE GREAT BARTHOLDI STATUE,
LIBERTY ENLIGHTENING THE WORLD.
THE GIFT OF FRANCE TO THE AMERICAN PEOPLE.
TO BE
ERECTED ON BEDLOE'S ISLAND, NEW YORK HARBOR.

The statue of bronze, 148 ft. in height, is to be mounted on a stone pedestal 150 ft. high, making the extreme height 298 ft. The torch will display a powerful electric light, and the statue thus present by night as by day, an exceedingly grand and imposing appearance.

PUBLISHED BY CURRIER & IVES, COPYRIGHT 1885, BY CURRIER & IVES, N.Y. 115 NASSAU ST. NEW YORK

THE GREAT BARTHOLDI STATUE,

LIBERTY ENLIGHTENING THE WORLD.

THE GIFT OF FRANCE TO THE AMERICAN PEOPLE.

ERECTED ON BEDLOE'S ISLAND, NEW YORK HARBOR.

The statue is of copper-bronzed, 148 ft. in height, and is to be mounted on a stone pedestal 150 ft. high; making the extreme height 298 ft. The torch will display a powerful electric light, and the statue thus present by night as by day, an exceedingly grand and imposing appearance.

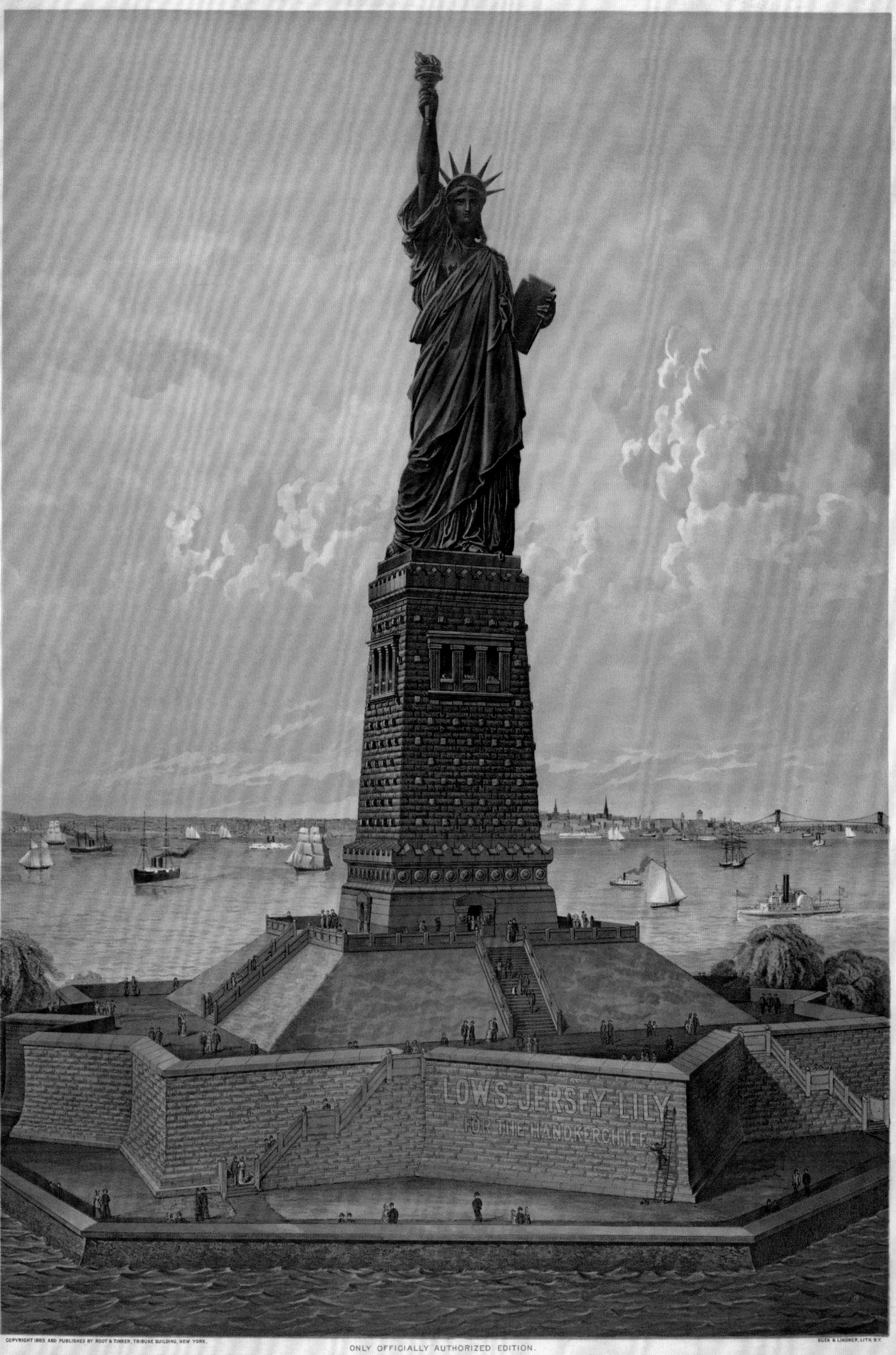

LOWS JERSEY LILY
FOR THE HANDKERCHIEF

ONLY OFFICIALLY AUTHORIZED EDITION.

LIBERTY ENLIGHTENING THE WORLD.

THE COLOSSAL STATUE BY BARTHOLDI.

PRESENTED BY THE FRENCH PEOPLE TO AMERICA.

As it will appear on its pedestal

ON BEDLOES ISLAND IN NEW YORK HARBOR.

HEIGHT OF PEDESTAL ABOVE HIGH WATER 177 FT. 9 IN. HEIGHT OF STATUE 151 FT. 2 IN. TOTAL HEIGHT FROM WATER 328 FT. 11 IN.

Jos. W. Drexel
CHAIRMAN
AMERICAN PEDESTAL COMMITTEE.

Bartholdi
SCULPTOR.

R. M. Hunt
ARCHITECT OF PEDESTAL.

The tribulations of the Statue of Liberty did not end with its official inauguration in 1886. In fact, the adventures concerning the reappropriation of its image had just begun.

Auguste Bartholdi understood the power of images, and used them for documentary purposes and to promote his work. His sculpture emerged at an opportune time, when advertising appeared in the United States and when the first illustrated newspapers and journals arrived on the market, all close to the event. Later, images of the statue were used for propaganda purposes and the sale of Liberty Bonds during the First World War. Graphic materials that were particularly aimed at tourists were also quick to appropriate the monument's image. Stamps and amateur souvenir photographs followed postcards. At the same time, the statue became a symbol of hope for immigrants arriving in the United States, cementing America as a welcoming land.

Almost as old as the sculpture itself, variations on the theme of the destruction of the statue and its annihilation were recurrent. These would reach a climax during the 1960s and 1970s through their depiction in popular imagery and science fiction.

Z.P. Nikolaki, *Hello! This Is Liberty Speaking — Billions of Dollars are Needed and Needed Now*, 1918. Color lithography, 12.2" × 9.1" (31 × 23 cm).
At the end of the First World War, Lady Liberty gained a place next to Uncle Sam, dethroning Columbia, who had long been the feminine symbol of America. During the first conflict, the term "liberty loan" helped propel the statue to the rank of national icon. Public borrowing campaigns intended to finance the war inevitably appropriated Liberty's image for their promotion. The first "liberty" lending campaign was launched with G.R. Macauley's poster, which depicted the statue pointing toward the observer with the caption, "*You buy a liberty bond.*" A year later, we find Liberty on the telephone calling for the collection of millions of dollars.

Liberty Is Ours

ELLO!

THIS IS LIBERTY SPEAKING—

BILLIONS OF DOLLARS ARE NEEDED AND NEEDED NOW

Unknown author, *The Great Bartholdi Statue: Liberty Enlightening the World with the World-renowned and Beautiful Star Lamp*, 1885. Lithography, tinted, 1885.
In the United States, Bartholdi's project was concomitant with the birth of advertisements that exploited the image of the promised statue, inflicting metamorphoses upon it ranging from partial substitution to total transformation. Before its American pedestal was finished, Liberty's torch had been subjected to several reinterpretations, here with an oil lamp instead of the torch.

Caricature by Frederick Burr Opper, *Let the Statue of Liberty Pay for its Own Construction Through Advertising*, 1885.
Before the pedestal was completed, advertisements were so abundant that the American satirical magazine *Puck* suggested, on April 8, 1885, to "Let the advertising agents take charge of the Bartholdi business, and the money will be raised without delay." Wearing sunglasses, holding a bottle of champagne instead of the tablet of law and an umbrella at the end of her torch, the statue was covered in slogans.

LET THE ADVERTISING AGENTS TAKE CHARGE OF THE BARTHOLDI BUSINESS,
AND THE MONEY WILL BE RAISED WITHOUT DELAY.

Unknown author, *Welcome to the Country of Liberty*, New York – scene of the bridge on the steamboat *Germanic*, passing by the Statue of Liberty, 1887. Engraving on wood.
If Lady Liberty emerged as a symbol of America, it was also because she represented its values: a land of welcome and the hope for a better life. The statue's association with immigration began in 1883 through the writing of Emma Lazarus, which added to the statue the dimension of being protector to the oppressed, "mother of exiles," and a beacon guiding immigrants searching for a new beginning.

"Give me your tired, your poor, / Your huddled masses yearning to breathe free, / The wretched refuse of your teeming shore. / Send these, the homeless, the tempest-tost to me, / I lift my lamp beside the golden door!"

Entitled *The New Colossus*, in reference to the Colossus of Rhodes, "with conquering limbs astride from land to land," this poem was featured in an exhibition that was designed to collect funds for the construction of the pedestal's construction before it was forgotten.

Rediscovered 20 years later, it was finally engraved in 1903 on a bronze plaque affixed to the base of the statue on Bedloe's Island. Today, immigrants no longer travel by boat around Liberty Island, but they are nevertheless greeted with Emma Lazarus' message, which is now inscribed at the arrival terminal at the John F. Kennedy International Airport.

American caricature of F. Victor Gillam opposing uncontrolled immigration, shown with the Statue of Liberty in New York being assaulted by immigrants, 1890.

The association of the Statue of Liberty with immigration was not initially planned. In fact, the 1886 inauguration speech warned immigrants that "there is place and a sense of fraternity for all those who wish to support our institutions and to contribute to our development, but those who come with the intention of disturbing the peace and violating our laws will forever remain strangers and enemies." In reality, and as immigration historian Maldwyn Allen Jones highlighted, the Statue of Liberty was inaugurated "at the time when Americans began doubting the benefits of uncontrolled immigration." These fears were notably expressed with the proposal to establish, in 1890, a new quarantine center for immigrants on Bedloe's Island. Denounced by Bartholdi as a "monstrous project," the idea inspired satirical illustrations such as this one, which depicted Liberty lifting her skirt to avoid being contaminated by the immigrants that spilled en masse at her feet. The Ellis Island immigration station began operating in January 1892, seven years after the statue was completed.

WINDOM
U.S. TREASURY
EUROPEAN GARBAGE-SHIP
EUROPEAN GARBAGE-SHIP
REFUSE

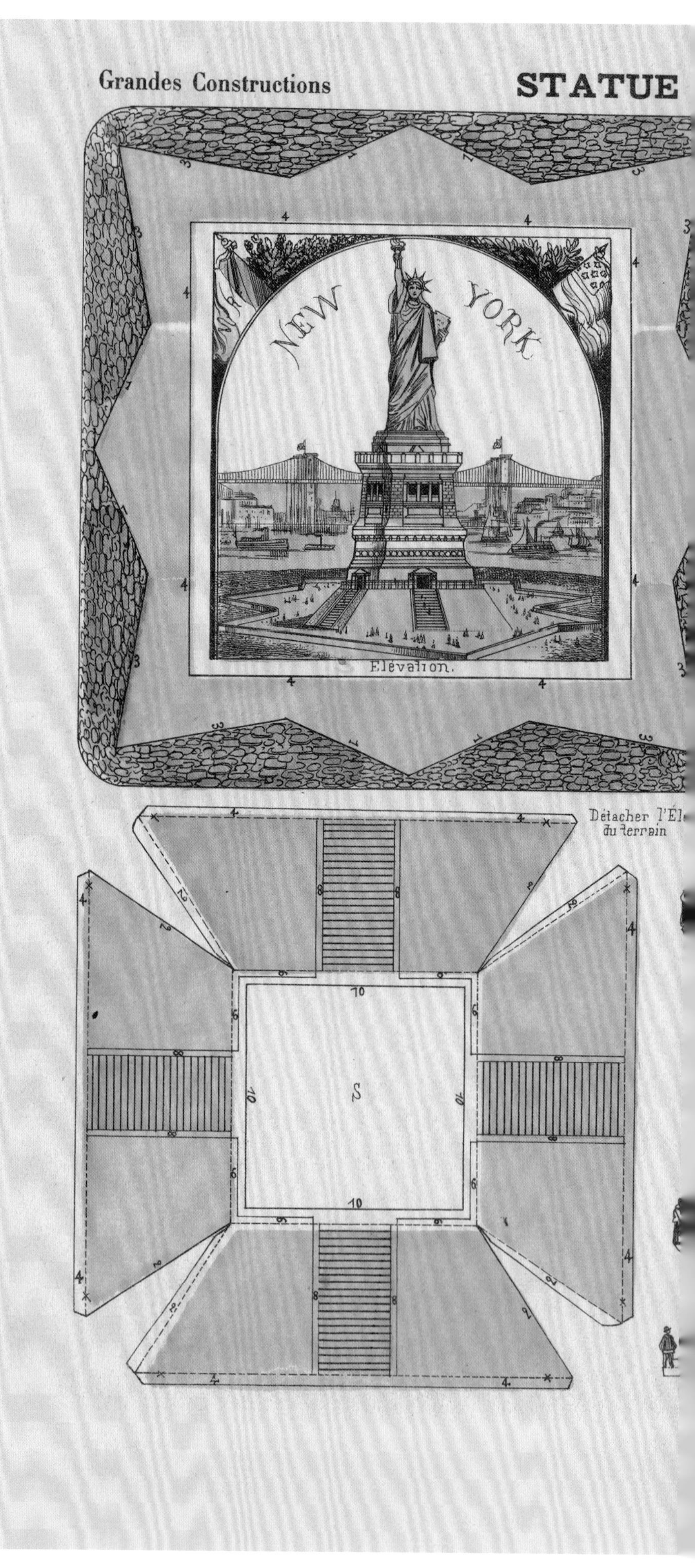

The Statue of Liberty, stencil lithography on cardboard (cutting board), 15.4" × 19.4" (39 × 49.3 cm). Épinal print, circa 1890.
Let each person build their own liberty. This was the proposal of the Imagerie d'Épinal, whose series "Grandes Constructions" has, since 1860, deconstructed famous world monuments such as the often ephemeral pavilions and palaces of the Expositions Universelles.. These do-it-yourself paper models offered a new form of possible appropriation of the statue and its image.

LIBERTÉ à New-York
IMAGERIE D'ÉPINAL, N° 417
PELLERIN
Entailler au dos toute ligne ponctuée marquée du signe X.

Lucien Jonas, *Four Soldiers — a Frenchman, an Englishman, an Italian and an American — with the Statue of Liberty*, 1918 (date represented in this picture is 1917), 28" × 21.3" (71 × 54 cm). Liberty, as drawn by military artist Lucien Jonas, stands in the background, a giant figure that is close yet far away. As in the poster by Sem (p. 145), Lady Liberty looks directly at the viewer, questioning his or her consciousness. It is not from the waves that she emerges, but from a piece of the land that has been invaded, where, in an allegory of brotherhood in arms, three soldiers are brought together: an Italian, an Englishman and a Frenchman. Standing tall between liberty and these men crushed by conflict, the American soldier, holding a fixed-bayonet rifle, brings the hope for victory.

Joseph Pennell, *That Liberty Shall Not Perish from the Earth, Buy Liberty Bonds: Fourth Liberty Loan*, 1918. Colored lithography, 40.9" × 29.5" (104 × 75 cm).

THAT LIBERTY SHALL NOT
PERISH FROM THE EARTH
BUY LIBERTY BONDS
FOURTH LIBERTY LOAN

2-8

HEYWOOD STRASSER & VOIGT LITHO. CO. N.Y. IMP.

Eugenie De Land, *Sunrise or Sunset: Own a Liberty Bond*, 1917. Drawing and watercolor, 39.7" × 29.9" (100 × 76 cm).

RIGHT PAGE

For the Liberty of the World, Subscribe to a Bank Loan at the National Bank of Credit, poster signed by Sem, 1917. Color lithography, 47" × 30.3" (119 × 77 cm).

During the First World War, the creation of the *Division of Pictorial Publicity* under the direction of the famous illustrator Charles Dana Gibson brought in contributions from hundreds of artists. Several propaganda posters depicted the motif of the Statue of Liberty in peril, under the threat of an enemy attack, fire or the risk of being engulfed by the waves if citizens did not actively participate in war efforts.

On the other hand, the poster by French artist Sem entitled *For the Liberty of the World, Subscribe to a Bank Loan at the National Bank of Credit,* depicted Liberty rising from the water against a peaceful horizon.

POUR LA LIBERTÉ
DU MONDE
SEM
Souscrivez à l'Emprunt National
À LA
BANQUE NATIONALE DE CRÉDIT

THE

THE AMERICAN
MIDDLE CLASS
Opportunity
J. OTTMANN LITH. CO. PUCK BLDG. N.Y.

TERS.

PREVIOUS PAGES

Carl Hassmann, *The Rising Waters*, in *Puck*, Vol. 59, No. 1527, June 6, 1906. Photomechanical print: offset, color.
A man, a woman and an infant dressed in rags — the "American middle-class" — are seated on the rock of "Opportunity" above the rising waters of "concentrated wealth," while sharks circle around them. Surrounded by the water, the Statue of Liberty holds her arm in the air like a call for help before drowning. This whistle-blowing atmosphere no longer had a place for advertisements that took creative liberties or satires that had the statue as a subject. The representations of Liberty drowning were premature. Considered as the first apocalyptic science-fiction films, *Deluge*, directed by Felix E. Feist in 1933, returned to this representation of the figure by showing a series of natural disasters destroying the East Coast of the United States, followed by a tsunami that ravages New York and destroys the Statue of Liberty.

PAGES 150–151

Freedom guides our steps.
Printed poster celebrating the Liberation, 12. 5" × 9.25" (32 × 23.6 cm).

Poster by the America First Committee, *War's First Casualty*, 1940.
Some posters from the Second World War revived the propagandist statements found on the iconographic material from the First World War and further served as warnings. For example, this poster shows a shell firing across the page and exploding Liberty's arm. The point was to encourage Americans to remain neutral. For the American isolationist pressure group at the roots of this campaign, Liberty would be the first victim of engagement in the war.

Joseph Udo Keppler, *Golden Cow Replaces Liberty*, 1912. Photomechanical print: offset, color.
In this illustration probably created by Udo, the son of Joseph Ferdinand Keppler, founder of Puck, Liberty has fallen from her pedestal and is drifting in the water, while in her place on the throne sits a "golden calf" in the light, crowned and adorned with a necklace bearing a dollar sign. Money and foolish behavior have here replaced liberty.

Le Président ROOSEVELT
Général Ch. de GAULLE
Maréchal STALINE
WINSTON CHURCHILL
Général EISENHOWER
Général de LATTRE de TASSIGNY
Maréchal MONTGOMERY
Général LECLERC
Maréchal JOUKOV
Général KŒNIG
LA LIBERTÉ GUIDE NOS PAS
Édition E. C. PARIS
MODÈLE DÉPOSÉ · TOUS DROITS RÉSERVÉS

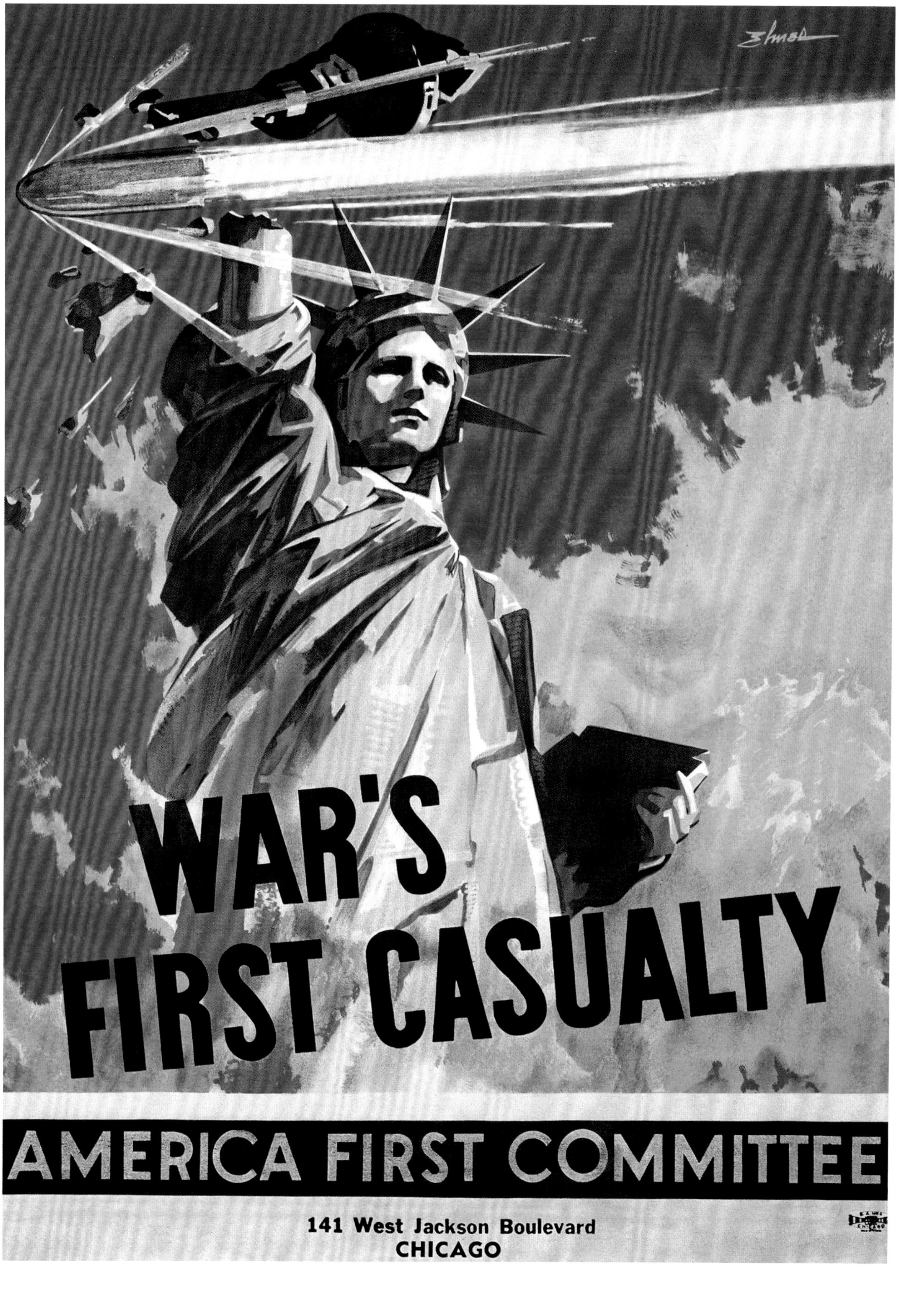

WAR'S FIRST CASUALTY

AMERICA FIRST COMMITTEE

141 West Jackson Boulevard
CHICAGO

Hubert Rogers, cover of *Astounding Science-Fiction*, 1941.

Earle K. Bergey, cover of *Startling Stories*, July 1942.

John Bowen, *After the Rain*, 1959. The figure of Liberty destroyed, buried or drowned accompanied the statue's symbolic adventure. It would often be referred to in science fiction, starting with Franklin J. Schaffner's film Planet of the Apes (1968). At the end of the movie, the heroes, who believe they are on another planet, come across the Statue of Liberty partially buried in the sand. The remains of the copper colossus confirm, without a doubt, that they are on planet Earth and all its humans seem to have been wiped out. Humanity as a whole is therefore represented by the mythical statue in this final sequence.

The destroyed or endangered figure that is Liberty is found in comics and on books or album covers. The motif is as prevalent as the innumerable appropriations of its image through advertisements, newspapers and propagandist material. This paradoxical association of the giant statue with decrepitude first appears the same year as its erection in New York. Yet its most unbridled parody helps to contribute to the original's prestige all while confronting it. During the years of 1965-1970, as is underscored by Philippe Roger, the multiplication of this iconoclastic effigy is the confirmation of the appropriation of the statue as a common reference: "The imaginary lesions on the mother nation, such as these graphic exactions, confirm, more solidly than the alliance iconography that was created during the times of war, the consecration of the 'mighty matron' as the totem head of the North American tribe".

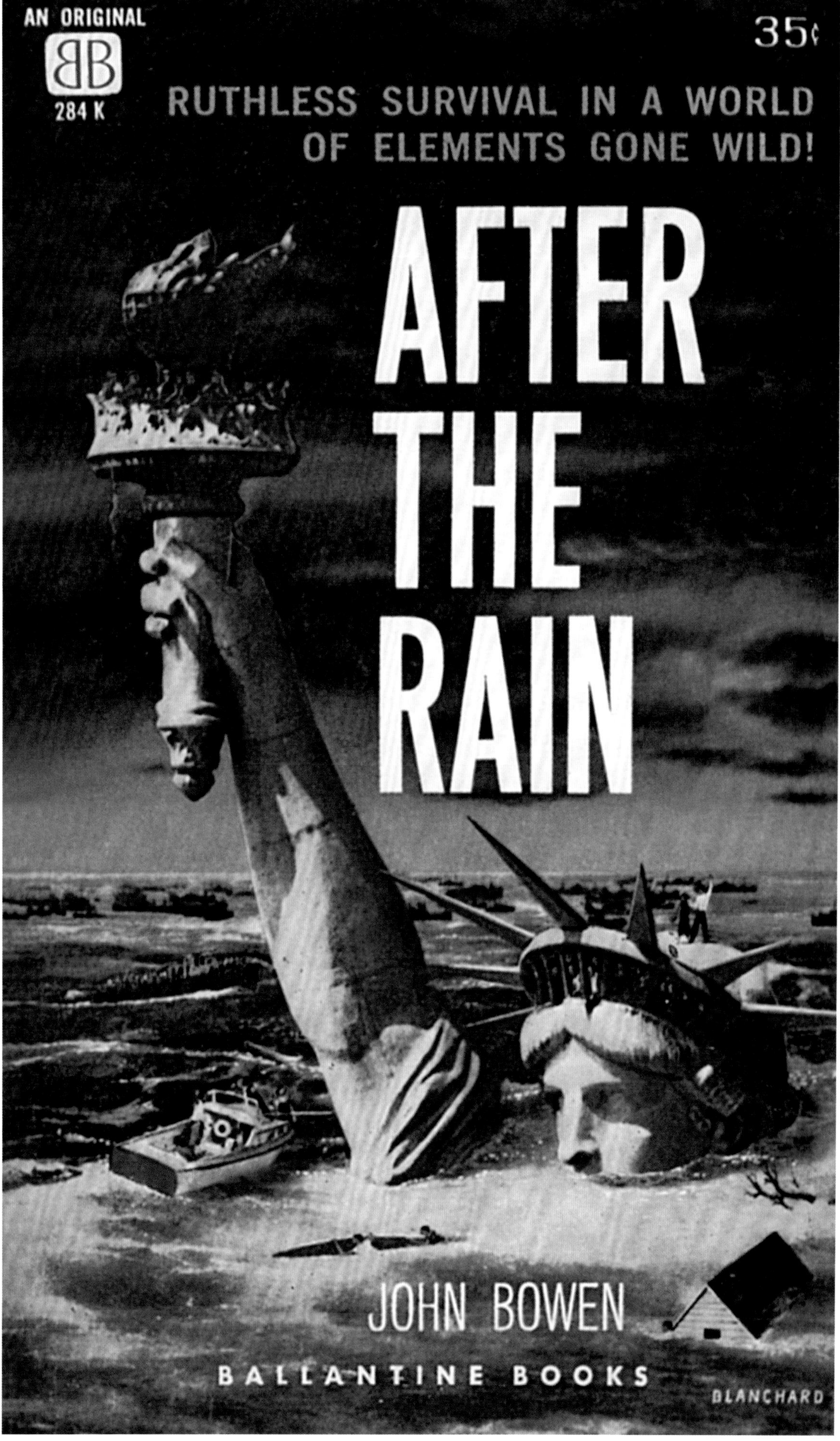
AN ORIGINAL
BB
284 K
35¢
RUTHLESS SURVIVAL IN A WORLD OF ELEMENTS GONE WILD!
AFTER THE RAIN
JOHN BOWEN
BALLANTINE BOOKS
BLANCHARD

Anonymous, "snapshots," second and third quarter of the 20th century, Jean-Marie Donat collection.
A pillar of the New York tourism industry, the "Lady of the Harbor" would come to adorn post cards, travel posters and souvenir guides. Here is a neat photomontage that seemingly allows the viewers to be placed next to the statue. Owning an image of oneself posing next to the Statue of Liberty is a definite way of making the statue one's own. To be photographed while holding the statue's pose, outfit and accessories is another form of the appropriation of this symbolic figure.

Arthur S. Mole and John D. Thomas, *Human Statue of Liberty; 18,000 Officers and Men at Camp Dodge, Des Moines, Ia; Col. Wm Newman, Commanding; Col. Rush S. Wells, Directing*, 1917. Photographic print.
This famous photograph features a human Statue of Liberty made up of 18,000 officers and men from from Camp Dodge in Des Moines. This statue made of flesh and blood was a literal incarnation of Liberty. It expressed the desire for symbolic appropriation of the monument, a desire to which the image and the products derived from it have contributed, and continue to do so.

Human Statue of Liberty
18,000 Officers and Men
at
Camp Dodge, Des Moines Ia.
Col. Wm. Newman, Commanding
Col. Rush S. Wells, Directing.
©
Mole & Thomas
915 Medinah Bld'g.
Chicago, Ill.

Bibliography

Aguila, Dani. *Taking Liberty with the Lady – By Cartoonists from Around the World.* Nashville: Eagle Nest Publishing Company, 1986.

Baboian, Robert, E. Blaine Cliver and E. Lawrence Bellante. *The Statue of Liberty Restoration.* Houston: National Association of Corrosion Engineers, 1990.

Bartholdi, Frédéric-Auguste. *The Statue of Liberty Enlightening the World.* New York: Allen Thorndike Rice, 1885.

Belot, Robert, and Daniel Bermond. *Bartholdi.* Paris: Perrin, 2004.

Berenson, Edward. *The Statue of Liberty: The History of a Franco-American Icon.* Paris: Armand Colin, 2012.

Berg, Shary P. *Cultural Landscape Report for Liberty Island, Statue of Liberty National Monument: History, Analysis and Treatment Recommendations.* Boston: Olmstead Center for Landscape Preservation, National Park Service, 1999.

Blanchet, Christian, and Bertrand Dard. *The Statue of Liberty: Centennial Book.* Paris: Diffusion Vilo, 1984.

Blumberg, Barbara. *Celebrating the Immigrant: An Administrative History of the Statue of Liberty National Monument, 1952–1982.* Boston: National Park Service, 1985.

Boime, Albert. *Hollow Icons: The Politics of Sculpture in Nineteenth-Century France.* Kent, OH: Kent State University Press, 1987.

Boime, Albert. *The Unveiling of the National Icons: A Plea for Patriotic Iconoclasm in a Nationalist Era.* Cambridge University Press, 1997.

Browne, Anita. *Golden Jubilee Poems of the Statue of Liberty.* New York: The Poets Press, 1936.

Burchard, Sue. *The Statue of Liberty: Birth to Rebirth.* San Diego: Harcourt, Brace, Jovanovitch, 1985.

Causel, Laurent. *Bartholdi and the Statue of Liberty: Centennial Commemoration.* Strasbourg : Éditions de la Nuée Bleue, 1984.

Claude Gauthier, *The Statue of Liberty: A Sign for You.* Paris: ABC, 1986.

Coffin, Margie, Charlie Pepper and Al Farrugio. *Statue of Liberty National Monument Landscape Preservation Maintenance Program.* Brookline, MA: Olmstead Center for Landscape Preservation, 1992.

Corcy, Marie-Sophie, Lionel Dufaux and Nathalie Vuhong. *The Statue of Liberty: Bartholdi's Challenge.* Paris: Gallimard, 2004.

Dillon, Wilton S., and Neil G. Kotler, *The Statue of Liberty Revisited: Making a Universal Symbol.* Washington DC: Smithsonian Institution Press, 1994.

Durante, Diane L. *Outdoor Monuments of Manhattan.* New York: New York University Press, 2007.

Gilder, Rodman. *Statue of Liberty: Enlightening the World.* New York: New York Trust Fund, 1943.

Gray, Walter. *Interpreting American Democracy in France: The Career of Edouard Laboulaye.* Newark: University of Delaware Press, 1994.

Grigsby, Darcy. *Colossal: Engineering The Suez Canal, Statue of Liberty, Eiffel Tower, and Panama Canal: Transcontinental Ambition in France and the United States During the Long Nineteenth Century.* Pittsburgh: Periscopic Press, 2011.

Griswold, William A. *Archeology of a Prehistoric Shell Midden, Statue of Liberty National Monument, New York.* Lowell, MA: National Park Service, 2002.

Griswold, William A. *Liberty Island, Archeological Overview and Assessment.* Lowell, MA: National Park Service Cultural Resources Center, 1998.

Grumet, Michael. *Images of Liberty.* New York: Arbor House, 1986.

Gschaedler, André. *True Light on the Statue of Liberty and Her Creator.* Narberth, PA: Livingston Publishing Company, 1966.

Haskins, James. *The Statue of Liberty: America's Proud Lady.* Minneapolis: Lerner Publications, 1986.

Hayden, Richard Seth, and Thierry W. Despont. *Restoring the Statue of Liberty: Sculpture, Structure, Symbol.* New York: McGraw-Hill, 1986.

Hill, Elizabeth Starr. *The Wonderful Visit to Miss Liberty.* New York: Holt, Rinehart & Winston, 1961.

Holland, F. Ross. *Idealists, Scoundrels, and the Lady: An Insider's View of the Statue of Liberty-Ellis Island Project.* Urbana: University of Illinois Press, 1993.

Hueber, Régis, and Christian Kempf, photographs. *Petite chronique imagée de la Statue de la Liberté.* Colmar: Musée Bartholdi, 2006.

Hueber, Régis. *Auguste Bartholdi, Designs ... Drawings: Preparatory Sketches of a Statuary*. Colmar: Musée Bartholdi, 1995.

Hueber, Régis. *From a Travel Album: Auguste Bartholdi in Egypt (1855–1856)*. Colmar: Musée Bartholdi, 1990.

Hugins, Walter. *Statue of Liberty National Monument: Its Origins, Development and Administration*. New York: National Park Service, 1958.

Kallop, Edward L. Jr. *Images of Liberty: Models and Reductions of the Statue of Liberty, 1867–1917*, New York: Christie, Manson & Woods, 1986.

Kaplan, Peter B., Lee Iacocca and Barbara Grazzini. *Liberty for All*. Wilmington, DE: Miller Publishing, 2002.

Khan, Yasmin. *Enlightening the World*. Ithaca: Cornell University Press, 2010.

Kinscella, Hazel. *Liberty's Island: Stories of the Harbor of New York, Bedloe's Island and the Statue of Liberty*. Lincoln, NE: University Publishing Company, 1947.

Lemoine, Bertrand. *The Statue of Liberty*. Brussells: Mardaga, 1986.

Marrey, Bernard. *The Extraordinary Life and Work of Monsieur Gustave Eiffel*. Paris: Graphite, 1984.

Moreno, Barry. *Statue of Liberty, Wonder of the World*. Impact Photographics, 2010.

Moreno, Barry. *The Statue of Liberty Encyclopedia*. New York: Simon & Schuster, 2000.

Moreno, Barry. *The Statue of Liberty*. Charleston, SC: Arcadia Publishing, 2004.

New York Public Library and the Franco–American committee for the celebration of the centenary of the Statue of Liberty. *Liberty: The French-American Statue in Art and History*. Edited by Pierre Provoyeur and June Hargrove. New York: Harper & Row, 1986.

Pauli, Hertha, and E.B. Ashton. *I Lift My Lamp: The Way of a Symbol*. New York: Appleton-Century-Crofts, 1948.

Perrault, Carole L. *The Statue of Liberty and Liberty Island: A Chronicle of the Physical Conditions and Appearance of the Island, 1871 to 1956*. Boston: National Park Service, 1984.

Perrault, Carole L. *The Statue of Liberty National Monument – Documents on the Construction of the Statue of Liberty, the Foundation, the Pedestal, and Lighthouse Establishment*. Lowell, MA: National Park Service, Building Conservation Branch, 1997.

Pousson, John F. *An Overview and Assessment of Archaeological Resources on Ellis Island, Statue of Liberty National Monument*. National Park Service, Denver Service Center, 1986.

Price, Willadene. *Bartholdi and the Statue of Liberty*. Chicago: Rand McNally, 1959.

Schmitt, Jean-Marie. *Bartholdi : A Certain Idea of Liberty*. Strasbourg : Éditions de la Nuée Bleue, 1986.

Schor, Esther. *Emma Lazarus*. New York: Schocken Book, 2006.

Shapiro, Mary. *The Statue of Liberty: The History of its Construction*. Paris: Flammarion, 1986.

Skomal, Lenore. *Lady Liberty, A Biography*. Kennebunkport, ME: Cider Mill Press, 2008.

Sutherland, Cara. *The Statue of Liberty*. New York: Barnes & Noble Books, 2003.

The Statue of Liberty: The Centennial Exposition, exposition catalog. Paris: Musée des Arts Décoratifs, 1987.

Trachtenberg, Marvin. *The Statue of Liberty*. New York: Viking Press, 1976.

Uschold, David. *Cultural Landscape Inventory, Liberty Island*. Boston: National Park Service, 1996.

Vidal, Pierre, and Christian Kempf, photographs. *Frédéric-Auguste Bartholdi, 1834–1904: Par l'esprit et par la main [By the Mind and By the Hand]*. Lyon: Les Créations du Pélican, 1994.

Weinbaum, Paul. *Statue of Liberty, The Story Behind the Scenery*. Las Vegas: KC Publications, 1988.

Chronology

1856
After having studied photography in Paris, Auguste Bartholdi undertakes, as a photography commission, a trip to the Middle East. His taste for colossal statuaries is affirmed during his visit in Egypt.

1865
Over the course of a dinner that the young Bartholdi attended, the Republican Édouard de Laboulaye suggests the idea building, in collaboration with the United States, a monument commemorating the American Independence. Auguste Bartholdi the sculptor then begins imagining the conception of a statue celebrating the event.

1867
Bartholdi worked over two years on the preparation of the beacon statue, *Egypt Bringing Light to Asia*, meant to adorn the entrance to the Suez Canal. Presented to the Khedive Ismaïl Pacha, the project did not did not however meet with the hoped-for success. Nevertheless, this statue, depicting a fellah brandishing a torch, predicts what would become the Statue of Liberty.

1870
Bartholdi produces the first Statue of Liberty model. Signed and dated, this first drawing measures 10.3" (25.75 cm) and is preserved today

1871
Incited by Laboulaye, Bartholdi undertakes a trip to United States with the goal of promoting their project. It is the ideal occasion for the sculptor to pick out the location for his future monument; Bedloe's Island.

1875
The Franco-American project receives its official name as "Liberty Enlightening the World," simultaneously with the creation of the Franco-American Union—which is presided over in France by Édouard de Laboulaye—and is tasked with raising funds in France and the United States to finance the statue. Designed by Bartholdi, a print depicting the statue of *Liberty Enlightening the World* at its future site accompanies the subscriptions. Work begins with the help of the architect and restaurateur Eugène Viollet-le-Duc.

1876-1884
The completion of the work and the erection of the statue are done in the Monduit plumbing and copper smelting workshops, Gaget, Gautheir & Co., located at 25 rue de Chazelles in Paris. Sheets of copper that were hammered to a thickness of 0.03" to 0.12" (0.75 - 3 mm) form the pieces of the giant puzzle that would come to weight a total of 88 tons (80 tonnes).

1876
The hand holding the flame, the Statue's first finished piece, was transported to the United States and presented at the World Fair in Philadelphia, then sent to Madison Square in New York. This is yet another occasion for Bartholdi to visit the United States. The gift of the Statue is accepted by the United States Congress, which officially declares Bedloe's Island as the monument's future installation site.

1878
The copper head is completed at the Parisian workshops and presented at the Exposition Universelles in Paris where it becomes one of the most popular attractions; it could be visited and created the opportunity for the distribution of souvenirs inspired by the head.

1879
After Viollet-le-Duc's death, the engineer Gustave Eiffel, suggests a completely different metal structure. Models of the Statue made of terracotta are circulated, signed and numbered.

1881
The American committee for construction of the Statue calls of bids to construct the base, despite Bartholdi already having completed several sketches. Architect Morris Hunt is chosen. He proposes the first project in 1882, while work on the true-to-size model at the Museum of Colmar. Measurement begins near the Parc Monceau in Paris.

1883
Ferdinand de Lesseps takes over the Franco-American Union presidency after Édouard de Laboulaye's death. The statue project inspires the poet Emma Lazarus to dedicate one of her works, *The New Colossus*, while work on the cement foundations begins on the pedestal.

1884
In France, President Jules Grévy officially presents the statue to the American Minister to France, Levi P. Morton. On the other side of the Atlantic, the lack of funds halts work on the pedestal construction site.

1885
Bartholdi publishes *The Statue of Liberty Enlightening the World*, the statue's history meant to promote the project, with the goal of helping the financing of the pedestal. The press would get involved, mocking but also helping the work on the monument; Joseph Pulitzer, editor of the newspaper *New York World*, thus manages to amass $102,000 after a thunderous national campaign. Dismantled in Paris, the Statue is transported in over 200 cases, on board a military ship named the *Isère*, which would reach the New York dockside four months later.

1886
The pedestal is finished, the definitive version of the statue assembled. The inauguration ceremony takes place on October 28, 1886.

Sources

The majority of the images and documents reproduced in this book originate from the Musée Bartholdi in Colmar, in the Alsace region of France. Established in 1907 thanks to Auguste Bartholdi's widow, who bequeathed her husband's childhood home to the town, this museum houses an important collection of plaster and terracotta models, as well as furniture that belonged to the sculptor. In addition to the numerous drawings and paintings, there are many photographs taken by Bartholdi himself during his travels to the Middle East between 1855 and 1856, as well as the collection of photographs that were the results of his personal documentation. The museum also retains numerous press clippings relating to the history of the construction of the Statue of Liberty, and an important collection of published articles on *Liberty Enlightening the World* from the illustrated press (*L'Illustration, Le Monde illustré*, etc.).

Some of the images found in this book, such as those of the construction of the pedestal in New York, are gifts donated by the sculptor's descendants to the library of the National Conservatory of Arts and Crafts, in Paris. These donations include Liberty models and, as in Colmar, French and American press clippings, engravings, photographs and other documents relating to the statue's construction.

In the United States, the Manuscripts and Archives Division of the New York Public Library holds the correspondence between Bartholdi and Richard Butler, secretary of the American Committee of the Statue of Liberty, while the Statue of Liberty National Monument maintains an important collection of photographs from the period, all relating to the Statue's construction in New York. The records concerning the activities of the American Committee are kept at the New-York Historical Society, while the archives of architect Robert Hunt — creator of the pedestal — can be found at the American Institute of Architects in Washington. The original drawings of the projects pedestal's various stages serve as companions to the prints depicting Eiffel's interior structure's elevation, and to the construction area photographs.

Finally, the Washington Library of Congress also houses some original photographs of the statue's assembly in New York, as well as several iconographic documents that attest to the various reappropriations of its image — some of which are reproduced in this work.

Acknowledgments

Gilbert Meyer, Maire de Colmar
Isabelle Bräutigam
Christian Kempf

Jean-Marie Donat

Patrick Pecatte
Gérard Lévy
Marie-Sophie Corcy

Claude Sintes
Fabrice Denise

Julie Héraut
Eline Gourgues

Ludovic Lebart
Gabriel Wegrowe

Index

G

H

I

R

S

T

U

V

W

Credits

Department of Archives Haut-Rhin, Colmar, reproduction by Christian Kempf: 14 bottom, 61, 69.
Colmar Public Library, reproduction by Christian Kempf: 12 left, 81.
Collection from and reproductions by Christian Kempf: 18, 113, 150.
Private collection: 152, 153.
Jean-Marie Donat: 154, 155.
Library of Congress, Washington: 4, 122–123, 125, 126–127, 128, 129, 130, 131, 134, 136–137, 142, 143, 144, 145, 146–147, 159, 157.
© Musée des Arts et Métiers-Cnam/ photo by Sylvain Pelly: 116–117, 119.
Musée Bartholdi, Colmar, reproduction by Christian Kempf: 10, 11, 15, 16, 17, 21, 27, 29, 31, 32–33, 34, 35, 36, 37, 40–41, 42–43, 44–45, 46–47, 48–49, 50–51, 52–53, 54–55, 56–57, 59, 60, 62–63, 64, 65, 67, 68, 71, 72, 73, 75, 76–77, 78, 79, 80, 82–83, 85, 86, 87, 88, 92, 93, 94, 95, 96, 97, 100–101, 102, 103, 104, 105, 109, 110–111, 121, 140–141.
Musée Unterlinden, Colmar, reproduction by Christian Kempf: 12 right, 39.
RMN-Grand Palais: Château de Blérancourt/Thierry de Girval: 14 top.
Roger-Viollet: Musée Carnavalet: 91; © Bilderwelt: 133.
Rue des Archives/© Granger NYC: 99, 107, 115, 135, 139, 152.

Acknowledgments

Gilbert Meyer, Maire de Colmar
Isabelle Bräutigam
Christian Kempf

Jean-Marie Donat

Patrick Pecatte
Gérard Lévy
Marie-Sophie Corcy

Claude Sintes
Fabrice Denise

Julie Hérault
Eline Gourgues

Ludovic Lebart
Gabriel Wegrowe

FRONT COVER

Albert Fernique, *Gaget, Gauthier & Co. Workshop: Construction of the Statue of Liberty*, Paris, 1884. Albumen print, 18" × 13"(46.2 × 33.4 cm).

BACK COVER

J. H. Beals, *Panorama of New York with bridge of Brooklyn under construction*, circa 1876. Panoramic Albumen print, in six parts, 13" × 103" (33.5 × 264 cm), detail.

ARLES
LES RENCONTRES DE LA PHOTOGRAPHIE

This book is the catalog of the Lady Liberty exhibition mounted at the Musée de l'Arles et de la Provence antiques, which took place from July 4 to September 11, 2016. The exhibition was organized in collaboration with the Bartholdi Museum, Colmar.